TORRE
during the
COLD WAR

Torrejón during the Cold War

History of Torrejón Air Base, Spain during the Cold War (1953 - 1992)

Manuel Carazo
José C. García González-Bárcena
Carlos Espinosa López

This book is dedicated to all the men and women who served at Torrejón Air Base and their families. Thank you for your service.

Contents

Preface

I want to start these lines with my sincere thanks to the authors of this fascinating book, for their distinction and confidence in giving me the opportunity to write a few lines about a book that deals with the history of an air base in which I have served for more than eleven years, and in which I had the privilege of commanding the 12th Wing, an emblematic unit of the Spanish Air Force that has been linked to Torrejón Air Base since its inception. It is an honor and personal satisfaction. Thank you very much Manuel, José and Carlos.

The importance and transcendence of Torrejón Air Base during the Cold War are faithfully reflected in the pages of this magnificent book. In the mid-fifties, and a few kilometers from Madrid, one of the most advanced air bases of that time was built, of joint Spanish-American use. For nearly four decades, Americans and Spaniards, military and civilians have worked on it, in harmony with which the relations between the two countries have been characterized

Torrejón Air Base was a direct consequence of the Madrid Pacts of the year 1953, a series of agreements by which three USAF air bases were installed in Torrejón, Zaragoza and Morón as well as a naval air station base in Rota, greatly influencing the society of the cities where they settled. Today, these bases built by the United States, remain fundamental for the security of Spain. Zaragoza, Torrejón and Morón are essential enclaves for the Air

Force, while at the Naval Base of Rota, the Navy houses the headquarters of the Fleet.

At present, the American footprint is still present in Torrejón, in which they had a direct relationship with it and its facilities. In addition to the aeronautical infrastructures, which have been adapted to current needs, they continue to be used almost without variation with respect to their original design, the chapel, the theater, the gym, the golf course, the bowling alley, the residences and the houses that were built in it. The presence of the USAF in Torrejón had an important influence on Madrid society, which became evident in the economic, cultural and sports fields.

The American Base as the inhabitants of Torrejón called it, always caused mixed feelings among the residents of the municipality. For some, its installation reported benefits; for others, it only contributed to generate problems for the citizens. But what everyone agrees is that for many years it influenced the personality of Torrejón de Ardoz. From then on, the image of Torrejón changed dramatically and its name crossed borders.

I am currently fortunate to be in command of the Zaragoza Air Base, whose history is linked to that of its sisters in Rota, Morón and Torrejón, and that in the same way has left an important mark on the Zaragoza society. With the arrival of the US military, Zaragoza approached new cultures and discovered hitherto unknown products, including hamburgers, Levi's jeans and American tobacco. The same goes for the base facilities, which continue to remind us daily of the American presence in it.

At the end of reading this interesting book about Torrejón Air Base and the Cold War, I can only wish that my friends Manuel Carazo, José C. García González-Bárcena and Carlos Espinosa López prepare a similar title on the Zaragoza Air Base.

Brigadier General **Antonio F. Nebot Mas**, SPAF
Commander Zaragoza Air Base
Former 12th Wing Commander, Torrejón Air Base

Foreword

It is a great honor to write the foreword for this wonderful book telling the history of one of the most important Air Force bases in Europe, Torrejón Air Base, Spain.

My dear friend Manny Carazo and his friends José C. Bárcena and Carlos Espinosa wrote this book to offer their perspectives and share the unique history and importance of Torrejón Air Base.

Torrejón Air Base had its beginnings in 1957 with the arrival of the Strategic Air Command (SAC) and its B-47 Stratojets bombers during the Reflex operation, a vital operation to avoid a possible attack by the former Soviet Union. This book, which begins in 1957 and ends in 1992, with the departure of the last aircraft assigned to the 401st FW, shares the unique and unprecedented history in detail. It also features fascinating and unique photographs, many of them never published before.

Why am I writing this foreward? I am not military personnel. I am a civilian. Fortunately, my deep relationship with Spain began in 2009 when my husband Alan was asked by President Barack Obama to be the United States Ambassador to Spain and Andorra. From our arrival in Madrid in 2010, we got to meet and know the wonderful men and women who represent our country in military service and those who support them. Manny Carazo is one of them. I met Manny as he was an essential part of our

US Marine detail. Manny is revered by both US and Spanish officers and military personnel. He has helped our Marine Corps detachment during the Marine Corps Birthday Ball and many other events, he also founded the Semper Brothers Foundation with his two friends Jose Bárcena and Carlos Espinosa, Manny is a person of many talents.

In Alan's role as Ambassador, we traveled to Torrejón many times. We were at Torrejón when Vice President Biden met with Spanish troops who fought alongside US troops in Afghanistan. It was at Torrejón where Secretary of State Hilary Clinton arrived to meet with members of Spain's Foreign Ministry. These are just two of are countless stories that can be told about Torrejón. It has a revered history and it's now being told in this book. Bravo to Manny Carazo for the extensive research and attention he gave to this book. It is a testament to his caring about the US, Spain and Torrejón.

Susan Lewis Solomont lived in Spain from 2010-2013 when her husband Alan served as US Ambassador to Spain and Andorra. Susan is the author of *Lost and Found in Spain Tales of An Ambassador's Wife*, a memoir and travelogue about her years in Spain and *Stella the Ambassadog*, a children's book about diplomacy as seen through the eyes of her dog Stella Blu.

Introduction

I have a unique perspective on the life of the F-16 at Torrejón Air Base, Madrid, Spain. On March 19, 1983, I flew in one of the first five F-16s to be assigned to the 401st Tactical Fighter Wing (TFW) at Torrejón, and on March 24, 1992, I flew out one of the last four F-16s to leave Torrejón as the 401st was deactivated in preparation for its move to Aviano Air Base, Italy. During that period, my family and I spent two, three-year tours of duty at Torrejón with another three-year tour at Ramstein Air Base, Germany, sandwiched in between.

But I didn't land at Torrejón Air Base on that March day in 1983!

That day began at approximately 1 AM US time when I took off from Shaw Air Force Base, South Carolina, as #3, the alternate flight lead, in a flight of five F-16s. The 8-hour flight, which included three inflight air refueling from an accompanying KC-135 tanker aircraft, was uneventful. We arrived over Spain on a beautiful, clear day. Number 2 (#2), a new F-16 pilot with just enough F-16 flight time to qualify to make the long, over water flight, was the first to identify Torrejón as we approached Madrid from the west northwest at about 15,000 feet.

Madrid Control vectored us north of the base, cleared us to descend to traffic pattern altitude, and handed us off to the Torrejón Air Traffic Control Tower. The flight lead (#1) echeloned the flight left and closed us up to a tight five-ship fingertip formation as we flew down initial to the break point near midfield. He signaled the break which we each executed at the previously briefed 5 second intervals.

As I rolled out of my break, I noted that spacing looked good between #1, #2, and me. I then concentrated on preparing for my upcoming landing: gear down and checked for three green lights, no red light in the gear handle, speed brake closed, backup airspeed calculated, and radio call complete. As I rolled out a mile on final at about 300 feet above ground, I reconfirmed that spacing still looked good between #2 and me. As #2 touched down in front of me, I immediately saw a bright red flash that looked like fire coming from the right side of his aircraft fuselage. Something was wrong. I immediate executed a go-around, raising my landing gear and directing #4 and #5 to executed go-arounds and rejoin on me. As I flew a right climbing turn back to pattern altitude, I saw that #2 was stopped halfway down the runway, angled slightly, and smoking a little. My three-ship was not going to land at Torrejón that day!

A quick check of my remaining fuel and that of my two wingmen told me that we would be emergency fuel if we diverted to the primary weather divert field of Zaragoza Air Base in northern Spain. I made the decision to divert to the nearest military base which was Getafe Air Base located in Southeast Madrid. I told Torrejón Tower my intensions. The Tower controller gave me a contact frequency for Madrid Control. Once I was in contact with Madrid, the controller cleared me and my flight of three F-16s direct to Getafe Air Base.... flying right across the commercial aircraft final approach path to Barajas International Airport!

As we approached Getafe, I contacted the Getafe Air Traffic Control Tower and asked for landing instructions. I do believe they were a bit surprised! After all, this was a Saturday, the air base was essentially closed for the weekend except for emergencies, and they had no planned arrivals, especially three F-16s which they had never seen before in Spain!

I quickly briefed my two inexperienced wingmen on the inter-flight VHF radio, reminding them of key safety items to be especially aware of landing at a strange airfield with a much shorter and narrower runway then the planned landing at Torrejón. I brought the flight down initial in a nice tight echelon right fingertip formation and pitched out. All three F-16s landed without incident. My junior wingmen did a great job.

As I taxied my flight to the de-arm area just off the north end of the runway, I became immediately concerned about possible foreign object damage (FOD) to our aircraft. It seemed like there were rocks everywhere on the taxiway! The F-16 engine is notorious for “vacuuming” up debris that comes in close proximity to its intake. I really didn’t want to damage our three-brand new F-16s, each of which was on only its fifth flight since it rolled off the assembly line at General Dynamics, Fort Worth, Texas! I alerted my two wingmen and we carefully avoided everything we saw. We were successful!

Given the FOD problem, I decided that we would just shut down in de-arm. Unfortunately, because of our surprise arrival, there was no one around to help us. Again, I briefed my wingmen on what we were going to do. Usually the F-16’s Emergency Power Unit (EPU), powered by a diluted version of highly toxic hydrazine - a rocket fuel - is rendered inoperative with a pin by the ground crew before the pilot shuts down the engine. This is a backup procedure in case the ground sensing switch on the aircraft is not working correctly. With a faulty ground sensing switch and no safety pin installed, the EPU will interpret the engine shutdown as an inflight engine failure and automatically activate. Not good on the ground!

We set our parking brakes and shutdown our engines. No EPU activated. We safetied our ejection seats, unstrapped, and, using the seat harnesses, let ourselves down from the cockpits to the ground. Once on the ground, we put in the handing gear safety pins and safety-pinned the EPUs.

Still no one was coming to our aid. I told my wingmen to find at least six large rocks we could use to "chock" at least one of each aircraft's main wheels so we could climb up to our cockpits and turn off the parking brakes. If we hadn't done that, the brake disks, compressed with the parking brakes on, could build up enough heat to activate the blow out plugs causing the tires to go flat and possibly starting wheel fires!

Mission accomplished, we sat down on the ramp to await our "rescue" and speculate what had happened to #2. In the meantime, I noticed dozens of cars stopping on the highway that ran just parallel to the de-arm area where our three F-16s were parked. Aviation enthusiast are the same everywhere! This was obviously a special treat for them as I doubt that any of those stopping had ever seen an F-16 before.

Finally, after about a half hour, I spotted a lone vehicle heading our way. My Spanish was, and is, rudimentary, at best. At least I knew how to say: “Donde esta el telephono?” I told my wingmen to “guard the jets” and rode with the driver to Getafe Base Operations where I called the 401st TFW Command Post. I told the controller that we were down safely and that the jets were all “Code 1”, in other words, ready to fly again.... except for some much needed JP-4 (gas). I was told that the airfield was closed, that things were chaotic there, and that help would be on the way....in several hours!

The driver returned me to the de-arm area where my wingmen and I settled in to await the Torrejón maintenance and security crews. We continued to speculate. Did #2 loose a wheel?, Did a tire blow?, Did the main gear collapse?, Did a fuel tank release?, Had the nose gear failed?.

Finally, the maintenance and security crews arrived. What happened, we asked? Response: It appears that the pilot forgot to put his landing gear down!! Wow! We never considered that!

So, my initial arrival at Torrejón Air Base, Spain, was via a van from Getafe Air Base! The next day, my wingmen and I returned to Getafe, started up our three F-16s, and flew them to Torrejón for a belated arrival!

Fortunately, my flight to Ramstein Air Base, Germany, in March 1992 was without incident or drama! Not only did I fly one of the last four F-16s to leave Torreon Air Base, it also turned out that I was flying my final flight in an F-16 and as an active pilot in the US Air Force. It was truly an end of two eras: The F-16 at Torrejón and my military flying career. I enjoyed both immensely!

Colonel **Wade L. Paton**, USAF (Retired)
Former Deputy Commander for Operations,
401st Tactical Fighter Wing

I was truly appreciative for the opportunity to have worked and interacted with a number of highly professional and well-respected senior members of the Spanish Air Force. This was particularly evident during the attempted coup in 1981. I can honestly state that my assignment to Torrejón Air Base was the best duty station of my entire military career. Icing on the cake was that my wife, Helen and I were honored to have met the King and Queen on several occasions.

Upon our return to the United States, my family and I would always say: "We may have left Spain - but Spain will never leave our Hearts. Que Viva España!

Gil Coronado, Colonel USAF (Ret)
401st Tactical Fighter Wing

Acknowledgments

The authors of this book want to thank Oscar Garza Solanas, Msgt USAF (Ret) Alex de Jesus, Major USAF Emma Piehl, Lauren Theodore, Archives Specialist, Archives II Reference Section (RDT2), HQ USAFE-AFAFRICA History and Heritage, Holly Reed National Archives & Records Administration Still Picture Reference Team, Doctora Rocío Piñeiro Álvarez, David Díaz "el viajero historico", Jim McCabe, Historian 307th BG Assoc. (www.307bg.net), Vicente Meneu via Javier Ballesteros, Roberto Yañez, Robert G. "Bob" Bradshaw, Jr., Colonel USAF (Ret.), Torrejón AFB, Spain Facebook page, US Armed Forces in Spain Facebook page, Ugo Gabbana, Air Force Historical Research Agency, Brigadier General Antonio F. Nebot Mas (Spanish Air Force), Roberto Lagunas Pison (President of AREA and ASNAPA), Miguel Angel Jimenez Arriero, Francisco J. Mendoza Dorado, Asociación Las Fotos de Torrejón de Enrique Sánchez Ferrera y Néstor Blasco Morena, Colonel USAF (Ret) Wade L. Paton, Ana Villareal Garza Paton, Susan L. Solomont, Colonel USAF (Ret) Gil Coronado, Mabel Minguez, Stars &Stripes and to all our family and friends to whom we have not been able to devote all the time we would have desired, for their patience and help.

Very special thanks to our friend and photographer, Carlos de la Cruz Avial (TJ SPOTTER), without his help and collaboration this book would not have come forward.

The Authors of **Torrejón during the Cold War**.

February 2020

Chronology

TORREJON AIR BASE

Torrejón Air Base was originally the home of the Spanish National Institute of Aeronautics, however following the Pact of Madrid of 26 September 1953, construction began at Torrejón on a new 13,400-ft concrete runway to replace the existing 4,266-ft grass airstrip and on a massive concrete apron and other necessary maintenance and shelter facilities to accommodate the largest United States Air Force bomber aircraft in the Strategic Air Command (SAC) inventory, with the base intended to support SAC Reflex missions.

USAF support activities began under the 7600th Air Base Group located in Madrid in July 1956, to support construction and base organizational functions. Torrejón Air Base opened officially on 1 June 1957 with SAC activating the 3970th Strategic Wing on 1 July 1957. The base hosting Sixteenth Air Force as well as SAC's 65th Air Division (Defense) where it cooperated with Spanish Air Force units in the Air Defense Direction Centers (ADDCs). The 65th Air Division directed base construction, and the establishment of off-base housing and radar sites. The division's fighter squadrons flew air defense interceptions over Spanish airspace. The division also controlled the operations of numerous attached tactical fighter squadrons that were deployed to Spain for temporary duty. Assigned or attached units of the division participated in numerous exercises with the Spanish Air Defense Command, and in some instances, with the U.S. Sixth Fleet.

In addition to the command and control mission, Torrejón Air Base hosted SAC reflex operations. Reflex operations consisted of rotating Boeing B-47 Stratojet wings overseas for extended duty as part of a dispersal program. Another reason for establishing Reflex bases was the relatively short range of the B-47, unlike the intercontinental range of the Convair B-36 "Peacemaker" and Boeing B-52 Stratofortress which could remain based permanently in the United States. Also, in this way SAC could spread out its potential as a Soviet target by placing its aircraft, weapons, and personnel on many more bases, with each bombardment wing having two additional installations to which it could disperse.

On 5 July 1958 the Air Defense Command's 497th Fighter-Interceptor Squadron arrived at Torrejón from Geiger AFB, Washington. It had an air defense role with North American F-86 Sabres. On 26 April 1960, the 497th FIS transitioned to the F-102 Delta Dagger and operated under SAC control until its transfer to the United States Air Forces in Europe (USAFE) 86th Air Division (Defense) at Ramstein Air Base West Germany on 1 July 1960. This transfer was made in order that all USAF fighter assets in Europe could be concentrated in one command. It operated F-102s until 3 June 1964, when it was reassigned to the 8th Tactical Fighter Wing at George AFB, California. Its F-102 aircraft were transferred to other USAFE 86th AD FIS squadrons.

Tactical Operations

With the phase out of the B-47 from SAC in the mid-1960s, the need for SAC European bases diminished. The Sixteenth Air Force was turned over to United States Air Forces Europe (USAFE) on 15 April 1966 and the strategic focus changed to tactical. Prior to 1966, Torrejón AB hosted TDY squadrons of tactical aircraft rotating from CONUS TAC bases which would perform 30-day rotations to Aviano Air Base Italy and Incirlik Air Base, Turkey.

With the USAFE takeover of the base, Tactical Air Command transferred the 401st Tactical Fighter Wing from England Air Force Base Louisiana to USAFE on a permanent basis to Torrejón on 27 April 1966, to perform host functions at the base and to support the rotational TDY duty to Italy and Turkey for NATO alerts.

The 401st TFW's initial operational squadrons at Torrejón were:

- 307th Tactical Fighter Squadron (1966–1971) (Tail Code: TJ)
- 353rd Tactical Fighter Squadron (1966–1971) (Tail Code: TK)
- 613th Tactical Fighter Squadron (1966–1993) (Yellow/Black Tails, Tail Code: TL)

401st TFW squadrons flew the North American F-100D/F Super Sabre.

Due to the demands of the Vietnam War, the 401st had deployed two of its three permanently assigned fighter squadrons (612th, 614th) to South Vietnamese bases (Phan

Rang AB, Phu Cat AB). To provide the 401st a full operational capability at Torrejón, aircraft and personnel were transferred on a permanent basis to the 401st TFW from Homestead AFB, Florida (307th TFS) and Myrtle Beach AFB South Carolina (353rd TFS).

As well as the USAFE tactical aircraft, SAC retained a presence at Torrejón with the 98th Strategic Wing flying Boeing KC-135 Stratotankers from the base. The 98th SW replaced the 3970th Strategic Wing on 25 June 1966. The 98th SW was inactivated at Lincoln Air Force Base Nebraska that same day with the closure of Lincoln AFB.

The 98th SW had no permanently assigned aircraft assigned, however CONUS-based SAC wings deployed aircraft to provide air refueling sup-port to meet the operational, alert, and exercise commitments of SAC, TAC, USAFE, and NATO in an area including the eastern Atlantic, most of Europe, North Africa, and the Middle East.

Even though neither were assigned to the base, when a B-52 and a KC-135 crashed off the coast of Spain in the 1966 Palomares B-52 crash, Torrejón became the focal point for the search for the missing nuclear weapons.

Military Airlift Command (MAC) operated the 625th Military Airlift Support Squadron at Torrejón to function as a major terminal for MAC transatlantic flights.

In 1970 the 401st TFW upgraded to the McDonnell Douglas F-4E Phantom II. In September 1973, an equipment change to the F-4C model took place, then in 1979 to the F-4D.

As a result of the withdrawal of USAF forces in South Vietnam, on 15 July 1971 the 307th and 353d fighter squadrons were returned to their home bases, and the 612th and 614th TFSs were assigned to Torrejón. Also in 1972, individual squadron tail codes were eliminated and "TJ" became the tail code for all 401st TFW aircraft.

On 31 December 1976 the 98th Strategic Wing was inactivated with its air refueling mission being taken over by the 306th Strategic Wing, based at Ramstein Air Base West Germany.

The 401st transitioned to the new General Dynamics Block 15 F-16A/B Fighting Falcon beginning with the first aircraft deliveries on 5 February 1983. The wing reached full F-16 operational capability on 1 January 1985. The F-16A/B models were upgraded to the Block 30 F-16C/D beginning in late 1987, with all aircraft replaced by September 1988.

Operational squadrons were:

- 612th Tactical Fighter Squadron (blue tail stripe)
- 613th Tactical Fighter Squadron (yellow tail stripe)
- 614th Tactical Fighter Squadron (red tail stripe).

Chapter I

THE PACTS OF MADRID

Introduction

In the following, the reader will be able to have a global idea of the position that Spain holds in the world, and its logical aspirations.

Fourteen years after the end of the Civil War in Spain, and eight years after the end of World War II, the Marshall Plan is in full development and operation throughout Europe, but Spain has been left out from receiving aid because of its support, albeit small, but support after all, to the fascist forces of the Axis; support that would not be withdrawn until the loss of North Africa from the Africa Korps of Nazi Germany and General Franco sees his aspirations diluted in North Africa: territories that Spain's Head of State has always longed for.

In the midst of the Cold War, which began in 1947, Spain has a clearly belligerent nature against communism, which places it politically in the western world, although its military dictatorship has already suffered severe setbacks and has been denied entry into the UN since nineteen forty-five, it therefore remains isolated from the western world.

Spain occupies a vitally important geostrategic place in the Cold War, at the entrance to the Mediterranean Sea, the only free exit door for the USSR Fleet from the Black

MADRID DOMINGO 27 DE SEPTIEMBRE DE 1953, NUMERO UNA PESETA

ABC

DIARIO ILUSTRADO AÑO CUADRAGESIMOSEXTO NUMERO 14.840

LOS GOBIERNOS DE ESPAÑA Y LOS ESTADOS UNIDOS FIRMARON AYER LOS CONVENIOS QUE REFUERZAN LA PREPARACION DE OCCIDENTE EN EL MANTENIMIENTO DE LA PAZ

Se prevé la construcción y uso conjunto por las dos naciones de instalaciones militares en nuestro país

EL GOBIERNO ESPAÑOL RECIBIRA AYUDA ECONOMICA, TECNICA Y MILITAR DE NORTEAMERICA

Los documentos fueron autorizados en Madrid por el ministro de Asuntos Exteriores, Sr. Martín Artajo, y el embajador norteamericano, Mr. Dunn

LAS INSTALACIONES Y BASES NAVALES Y AEREAS ESTARAN BAJO EL MANDO Y SOBERANIA DE ESPAÑA

MAC CARRAN EXTERIORIZA SU SATISFACCION, Y DICE QUE EL ACUERDO DEBIO FIRMARSE HACE VARIOS AÑOS

Era ir contra la realidad establecer la defensa de Europa sin contar con España, y el Ejército francés —afirma el mariscal Juin—se halla satisfecho por lo que se ha hecho ahora

En el Salón de Embajadores del Palacio de Santa Cruz se verificó ayer la solemne ceremonia de la firma, por los representantes de los Gobiernos de España y los Estados Unidos de América, de los tres Acuerdos entre ambos países.

Desde mucho tiempo antes de las cuatro de la tarde, el Ministerio de Asuntos Exteriores se hallaba invadido por numerosísimos periodistas nacionales y extranjeros, fotógrafos y operadores del "No-Do". Estos últimos habían preparado sus baterías convenientemente en el Salón de Embajadores, para el momento de la firma. A las cuatro se hallaban ya en el Ministerio los miembros de la Misión norteamericana, que fueron recibidos por el subsecretario del Departamento, señor Navasqüés, y el alto personal del mismo. Seguidamente llegó el embajador de los Estados Unidos en España, Mr. Dunn, que pasó al despacho del titular de la car-

EN ESTE NUMERO

El Padre Santo instaura, por la Encíclica "Fulgens Corona", un año mariano especial—que comenzará el 8 de diciembre—para conmemorar el primer centenario del dogma de la Inmaculada

(Pág. 39)

The governments of Spain and the United States signed the agreements for peacekeeping yesterday. **ABC** newspaper (Madrid). September 27, 1953

REDACCION Y ADMINISTRACION: Pelayo, 28

LA VANGUARDIA ESPAÑOLA

SUSCRIPCION

Precio de este ejemplar: 1 pta.

Domingo, 27 de septiembre de 1953

DOS GENERALES INVICTOS EN NOMBRE DE DOS GRANDES PUEBLOS

Acuerdo de España y Estados Unidos para el mantenimiento de la paz y de la seguridad internacional

Ayer, en el Palacio de Santa Cruz, fué subscrito en representación de España por el ministro de Asuntos Exteriores, señor Martín Artajo, y en representación de Norteamérica por su embajador Mr. James C. Dunn

El Acuerdo consta de tres protocolos sobre construcción y uso conjunto de determinadas instalaciones militares, aportación económica y ayuda para la organización defensiva de España

Las zonas e instalaciones para la utilización conjunta de España y Norteamérica, quedarán siempre bajo pabellón y mando español

La firma del histórico documento

Agreement between Spain and the United States for the maintenance of peace and international security. **La Vanguardia** Española newspaper (Barcelona). September 27, 1953.

Sea and rear-guard of the border with countries of Soviet influence.

At the same time, and after deep political-social cleansing in Spain, with the 1940s being a truly disastrous decade for the Spaniards, the country begins to stabilize and grow an incipient economy, creating a large working class that immigrates to the big cities, the Industrialization and urbanization of which creates countless jobs.

The United States is no stranger to Spain's growth, it's more political and highly important military officers conclude that it is perhaps a mistake that Spain is denied entry into the UN because of its past support for the Axis; Neither is the USA a stranger to the need for financial support in order to consolidate the growth of the industrial fabric and, at the same time, its strategic position in the Westernmost Mediterranean sea...

The Pacts

In nineteen forty-seven, a new conviction and more sanctions on the dictatorship of General Franco are proposed at the UN, but there is a turn of vital importance that would change the course of Spain from this moment on. The United States opposes these new sanctions, the immediate result of this is the opening of borders with France and the signing of trade and economy agreements with the United Kingdom and France.

In June of nineteen fifty, the first war since the cold war begins, the Korean War, initiated by the invasion of North Korea (communist regime) into South Korea (the Western block). Franco's regime informs the US of its

General Franco and President Eisenhower greeting each other upon arrival at Torrejón base. December 21, 1959

President Eisenhower and General Franco. December 21, 1959

condemnation of this invasion and its willingness to send Spanish troops to fight the communist regime. Spain was clearly contrary and belligerent to this type of political system.

This step taken by Spain, along with the American strategic interests that we shall see, subsequent to the step taken by the United States of America, led to the difficult and discreet initiation in Madrid of bilateral contacts in the year nineteen fifty, which were made difficult during the first stages by President Harry Truman's reluctance, although they were later unblocked with the arrival of President Dwight Eisenhower to the United States Presidency of the United States.

Spain wished to sign a Treaty with the US, but the Senate in Washington would have opposed it, since most of its members refused to support Franco's military dictatorship; this is why everything remained in an Executive Pact between governments.

The aforementioned Pact was signed on September twenty-third of nineteen fifty-three in Madrid, this is why they are called "The Pacts of Madrid," It was signed by Martín Artajo, Foreign Minister and James Clement Dunn, US Ambassador to Spain.

What were the Pacts?, The Pacts of Madrid consisted of three bilateral agreements: mutual defense, economic cooperation and technical assistance. The reader should not confuse The Pacts of Madrid with an extension of the Marshall Plan to Spain, applied in the belligerent European countries of World War II, this Plan was grant aid and only a small part of the Pacts of Madrid

Greeting the national anthem. Torrejón. December 21, 1959

Speech by General Franco. Torrejón. December 21, 1959

(about 20%) were in grants, the rest was to pay for building bases, to pay personnel and for military equipment. Although this will later be analyzed more specifically.

The economic contribution for the ten years that the first agreement lasted (1953 - 1963), is estimated at about one thousand three hundred million dollars, although there is information that even speaks of about one thousand five hundred million; based mainly on the aforementioned in the previous section and on purchases of surplus products from the United States of America, such as milk, cheese, cotton and coal, among others, as well as agricultural machinery.

As it has been previously mentioned, the aid was conditional, there were some percentages (initially quite high), established for spending on the bases, on military material and in industry.

As a result of the development of the Pacts of Madrid, the Rota naval base and the Morón and Zaragoza air bases are built and on which we are currently focused, in the vicinity of Spain's capital, the **Torrejón Air Base**.

In the economic section it is worth noting that although there is already a fledgling autonomous industry; The Pegaso truck factory in 1946 and the SEAT car factory, in May 1953, used for the development of ports and industrial areas in large cities. Proof of this is in the opening of the Citröen factory in Vigo (Pontevedra), in nineteen fifty-eight and also the Land Rover Santana factory in Linares (Jaén) in the same year.

At times of greater capacity and movement of troops, aircraft and ships, it is estimated that about 20,000 were

Speech by American President Eisenhower. Torrejón. December 21, 1959

General Franco and President Eisenhower review the troops. Torrejón. December 21, 1959

stationed or in transit on Spanish soil, including US military and civilian technical support personnel; not only in the four main bases, but also in other small installations of diverse use.

Although this has nothing to do with the Pacts, but so readers can have a broader view of the historical time, they should be informed that General Franco's Government receives the backing of the Concordat signed with the Catholic Church on August twenty-seventh of that same year, nineteen fifty three; The Concordat, together with the Pacts and subsequent bilateral agreements, gives Franco important international recognition, which leads to the entry of Spain into the UN on the fourteenth day of December, nineteen fifty-five, with thirty-eight votes in favor, ten against and twelve abstentions

Although the year of entry into the UN is 1955, this entry was forged after a very important diplomatic activity,

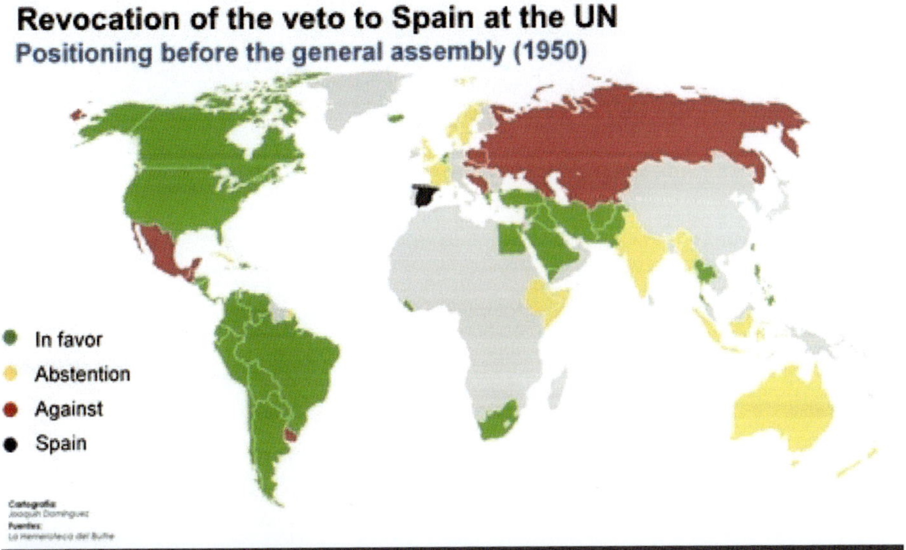

Voting map for the entry of Spain into the UN

President Eisenhower greeting Spanish authorities. December 21, 1959

Both dignitaries touring Madrid. December 21, 1959

which leads to United Nations General Assembly Resolution 386, dated November 4, 1950 and which is de facto “the beginning of the end” of international isolation for Spain, which began in 1945 after entry into the UN was denied.

Apart from this diplomatic activity, the Cold War was the main priority of the US authorities, to prepare plans, agreements or strategies to be ready in the event of war breaking out with the USSR. One of the most important was the Dropshot Plan, which emerged in late 1949, and for which they needed the help of European countries; for this, they had to recover financially after World War II, and the Marshall Plan emerged from there. This is the work of the Secretary of State, General George C. Marshall, and it was granted twelve billion dollars to help rebuild Europe, essentially for Britain, France, Germany, Italy, Belgium and the Netherlands. This is how the Americans sought to stop the advance of communism.

As previously stated, on September 26, 1953, James Clement Dunn, US ambassador to Spain, and Alberto Martín Artajo, Minister of Foreign Affairs, signed three agreements in the Palace of Santa Cruz, Madrid: one that was quite extensive on economic aid; another that was brief on defense and one on mutual defense aid.

Therefore, both nations established a commitment to the defense of international peace and security against the "communist danger". The defense agreement was the most important of the three, since it meant the establishment of US bases on Spanish territory. For the Americans, these military installations were indispensable for the strengthening of their strategic device, however Spain

Arrival at the Paseo de la Castellana of General Franco and President Eisenhower, Madrid. 21 December, 1959

Both dignitaries arriving at dinner at the Palacio de Oriente. 21 December, 1959

could not afford their construction or defense; so the regime had to be supplied with economic and military aid.

The Minister of Foreign Affairs, Martín Artajo, dealt with the study and negotiation of the diplomatic, political and legal aspects of the agreements. Military matters were dealt with by the General Chief of Staff, Lieutenant General Juan Vigón, and economic affairs by the Minister of Commerce, Manuel Arburúa. And on the American side the weight of the pacts was dealt with by the USAF General August Walter Kissner.

At first, the Americans only wanted the granting of territory where they could install their own military bases that could be temporarily used by their troops. The Spanish authorities hoped that in case of an external aggression they could use the Bases that had previously been prepared, thanks to the technical and financial assistance of the US.

Spain needed an army capable of dealing with potential "communist dangers", as well as aviation and naval improvements, given the great extent of their coast. The economic aid that Spain received in 1953 amounted to $ 226 million, including the 125 million granted between 1951 and 1952. The distribution of the total of this amount was 141 million dollars for military expenses and the remaining 85 to economically strengthen the military cooperation programme.

Regarding the Agreement on Economic Aid, it should be noted that Spain undertook to stabilize the currency, balance budgets, maintain financial stability, promote competitiveness and productivity, develop international

General Franco addresses guests at the Gala dinner at the Palacio de Oriente. December 21, 1959

President Eisenhower addresses guests at the Gala dinner in his honor at the Palacio de Oriente. December 21, 1959

trade and, in general, to do everything possible to keep the economy healthy.

In order to make more effective use of this economic aid, the International Commission was created where, under the chairmanship of the Spanish Minister of Trade, all undersecretaries of the ministerial departments of an economic nature participated and, as an executive body, the new Directorate General for Economic Cooperation of the Ministry of Trade was in charge of implementing the Agreement.

With regards to the Agreement on aid for Mutual Defense between Spain and the USA, to begin with, we will simply say that it bore similarities to those arranged by the latter with other countries in Europe and America.

Spain received financial aid through three different channels: the aid itself, the Public Law 480 funds and those from the so-called "McCarran Amendment".

It is very important to establish these differences, since the funds received came with very different conditions. The first thing to note is the nature of the aid and what exactly the American aid consisted of. The aid funds were not, as is often mistakenly thought, grant aid donations. Neither were they entirely loans. They were a mixture of both, they were partly loans and partly donations.

In the case of Spain, a good part of American aid consisted of granting loans with interest. Here we find a major first difference with the Marshall Plan. The aid received by Western European countries, under the coverage of this Plan, was mostly donations. The treatment

General Franco and President Eisenhower review the troops. Torrejón. December 22, 1959

General Franco dismisses President Eisenhower, on his right, John Davis Lodge, U.S. Ambassador, behind the Ambassador, his wife and General Minister of Air José Rodriguez. December 22, 1959

that Spain received was, in this sense, worse than that received by Italy, Germany or France, which is understandable given the background to which we have previously referred.

Another facet to take note of about the aid is that it generated what were called "counterpart funds". These funds were the value in pesetas of the dollar amount of the aid. The Spanish government had to make part of the funds coming from aid available in pesetas to the USA government, to meet its expenses in Spain, among which included expenses related to the building of the bases. To put it simply, part of the American aid was destined to meet the military and economic needs of the Americans in Spain.

Concerning the aid itself, 60 percent of the counterpart funds corresponded to the US government to finance the building of the military bases. Another 10 percent was also allocated to the US government to meet its administrative expenses in Spain. The remaining 30 percent, finally, corresponded to the Spanish government, as a donation; to be invested in transportation, communications and defensive industries with the approval of the US authorities. From 1958-59 the distribution of funds improved substantially in favor of Spain (up to 90 percent), as well as in the freedom granted to the government for its use.

The counterpart funds generated by the "McCarran Amendment" were distributed as follows: 80 percent for the Spanish government and 20 percent for the North Americans. However, unlike what occurred with the aid, the amount allocated to Spain was only a donation of 43.63 percent, the remaining 36.36 percent being a loan.

In relation to Public Law 480, distribution was approximately equal and the part corresponding to Spain was also a loan.

Another feature of the aid was that it was conditional. These were not funds that the Spanish government had full freedom to use. Part of the aid, such as all donations and a good part of the loans, were organized primarily according to American interests. This was the case with donations of food products and with loans granted for the purchase of agricultural products, which allowed US agricultural surpluses, particularly cotton surpluses, to be disposed of, thus yielding to the pressures that the US government was receiving from entrepreneurs in the cotton sector.

With all of this, when the Torrejón Air Base begins its journey, Spain is at full economic, industrial and military force, as it began to renew some armies and fleets that had completely obsolete material and in many cases that had come from Nazi Germany.

WELCOME TO TORREJON AIR BASE

Chapter II

16TH AIR FORCE

The Sixteenth Air Force came into existence on 16 July 1956. Even though the headquarters and command had no previous peacetime or wartime record, its lineal predecessor was the Joint United Sates Military Group (JUSMG), Air Administration (Spain), established in Madrid on 20 May 1954 by the direction of Headquarters, United States Air Force (USAF). JUSMG, Air Administration (Spain), had as its mission directive "to administer Air Force personnel on duty with Joint United States Military Group, Spain, and to provide area administrative jurisdiction over U.S. Air Force personnel in Spain." The new headquarters was directly subordinate to the Chief of Staff of the Air Force (CSAF) and had the procedural functions and responsibilities of a major air command. Its raison d'etre was to implement the U.S. - Spanish Defense Agreement of 26 September 1953, which authorized the U.S. to construct and operate air bases in Spain. The key Air Force representative in Spain during this period was Major General August W. Kissner, who negotiated the original agreement and was the first Chief, Joint United States Military Group, Spain. He also assumed command of JUSMG, Air Administration (Spain) and was Sixteenth Air Force's first commander.

Headquarters USAF first planned to move the 5th Air Division from French Morocco to Spain in order to operate the Strategic Air Command (SAC) bases to be created there, but later decided on a numbered air force (NAF) as the appropriate organizational level. The first choice, Sixth Air Force, was not available since it had been redesignated as Caribbean Air Command in 1946. Consequently, the Air Staff selected Sixteenth Air Force. Accordingly, on 16 July 1956, USAF redesignated Headquarters JUSMG, Air Administration (Spain), as Headquarters Sixteenth Air Force. The organization was assigned directly to the CSAF as a Special Operating Agency (SOA) and retained the same basic mission as its predecessor. General Kissner, who also continued to serve as Chief, JUSMG, Spain, began preparing for the SAC mission in Spain. Sixteenth Air Force assumed command responsibility for each base as it neared completion. The first to activate was Zaragoza Air Base (AB), on 14 February 1956, with the 7603d Air Base Squadron (ABS) as the host unit. Both Morón and Torrejón ABs were activated on 1 June 1957 with their initial host units being the 7202rd and 7600th Air Base Groups (AGB), respectively.

Upon completion of base construction in Spain, Headquarters USAF reassigned Sixteenth Air Force to SAC to be effective on 1 July 1957. Major General Henry K. Mooney took command of Sixteenth Air Force at its downtown Madrid headquarters, while General Kissner retained his position as Chief, JUSMG, Spain. Headquarters SAC replaced the old Sixteenth Air Force host units in Spain with new designations: the 3970th ABG at Torrejón, the 3973rd ABG at Morón, and the 3974th ABS at Zaragoza. Headquarters, Sixteenth Air Force moved to

Torrejón on 1 February 1958, and its bases became fully operational shortly thereafter. Strategic Air Command's Operation Reflex Rotational B-47 alert program began at Zaragoza on 29 May 1958, and at both Morón and Torrejón in July 1958. Sixteenth Air Force gained another unit on 8 April 1957 when SAC activated the 65th Air Division (Defense) at Torrejón AB. The air division assumed command of a seven-site aircraft control and warning (AC&W) system and three fighter interceptor squadrons to provide air defense of Spain. Later, United States Air Forces in Europe (USAFE) took responsibility for all air defense activities in the theater and assumed command over the 65th Air Division on 1 July 1960.

With its assignment to SAC, Sixteenth Air Force assumed command of SAC units and bases in Morocco in early 1958. The major SAC unit in Morocco, the 5th Air Division, was replaced on 15 January 1958 by the 4310th Air Division, which was assigned directly to Sixteenth Air Force. Under the division were the 3926th ABG at Ben Guerir AB, the 3906th ABG at Sidi Slimane AB, and the 3922rd ABG at Nouasseur AB. All three of these units were later redesignated as Combat Support Groups (CSG) under a 1959 SAC-wide reorganization plan. Air Material Command's 3153d Air Base Wing (ABW) at Nouasseur handled logistical support in Morocco, while USAFE's 316th Air Division (Defense) at Rabat provided air defense. The Moroccan bases, some of which had hosted SAC rotational bomber units since 1951, went on B-47 Reflex alert beginning with Sidi Slimane in July 1957, to be followed by Ben Guerir and Nouasseur in February 1958.

Sixteenth Air Force's primary mission until 1965 was to support and conduct SAC strategic operations from its bases in Spain and Morocco and from its ground detachments at such locations as Adana AB, Turkey, in an area which encompassed almost one quarter of the earth's surface. In addition to the Reflex B-47s, Sixteenth had operational control of B-52s and B-58s on airborne alert as well as rotational KC-135 tanker aircraft stationed at its bases to support such deployments.

Coincident with this period of intense mission activity, Sixteenth Air Force implemented mandatory base closures and budget cuts. The fact that the Reflex force in Spain, Morocco, and England helped face down the Soviets in both the 1961 Berlin and the 1962 Cuban missile crises had no effect on the future disposition of the bases. Having gained independence from France, Moroccan King Mohammed V insisted that the U.S. withdraw from all Moroccan bases. In a December 1958 meeting at Nouasseur AB, President Dwight D. Eisenhower personally met with the king and promised to close the bases by the end of 1963. After a period of nearly five years, the bases were closed in December 1963, as promised. At the same time, the U.S. retained the Spanish bases for another five years through the renewal of the 1953 agreement. In order to help secure the agreement's renewal, the U.S. promised to provide a wing of F-104 aircraft to the Spanish Air Force.

Also, in 1963, after the U.S.-Spanish base rights agreement was renewed, USAFE responded to Kennedy Administration Project Clearwater budget cuts by turning the Spanish air defense system over to the Spanish Air Force on 1 July 1964 and inactivating the 65th Air Division (Defense) on 1 January 1965. Headquarters SAC followed suit with the closeout of its B-47 Reflex operations at Zaragoza on 29 May 1964, at Torrejón on 31 March 1965, and at Morón on 1 April 1965. The impact of the end of Reflex operations was minimal given that the B-47s were being phased out of the Air Force active inventory, and their targets were assigned to B-52s, theater tactical air forces, and U.S. Navy Polaris submarines.

Thus, by the end of 1965, Sixteenth Air Force saw its peacetime mission responsibilities greatly reduced. Nonetheless, the Spanish bases retained an important role in wartime operations planning. In addition, KC-135 tankers continued to operate out of Torrejón with the task of refueling airborne alert B-52 and B-58 bombers in the European area. Unfortunately, it was during such a routine refueling operation on 20 January 1966 that a B-52 carrying nuclear weapons collided with a KC-135 tanker in mid-air. Both aircraft crashed near the small village of Palomares on the southeastern coast of Spain, and U.S. forces made an immediate effort to carry out recovery and cleansing actions. The ensuing operations, directed by the Sixteenth Air Force commander, to recover radioactive material and the "lost" nuclear weapon from the sea gained worldwide attention and profoundly affected U.S. - Spanish long-term relations.

Assignment to USAFE

It was under the shadow of Palomares that the Air Force announced the assignment of Sixteenth Air Force from SAC to USAFE, to be effective on 15 April 1966. The 401st Tactical Fighter Wing (TFW) equipped with F-100 fighters, moved from its U.S. base to Spain to take command of Torrejón AB and to assume the North Atlantic Treaty Organization (NATO) alert commitment at Incirlik Air Base, Turkey. The alerts were formerly manned by rotational elements (ROTE) from Tactical Air Command (TAC).

Third Air Force and Seventeenth Air Force assumed similar commitments at Aviano AB, Italy, and Cigil AB, Turkey, respectively. As of April 1966, Zaragoza AB was placed in "modified caretaker" status and administered by the newly designated 7472d Combat Support Squadron (CSS). Morón was retained as an active training base run by the 7473d Combat Support Group (CSG). Because of its assignment to USAFE, all of Sixteenth Air Force's four-digit subordinate units were redesignated from a 3900 series nomenclature to a 7400 series, as was the case with Morón's 3973d CSG, which became the 7473d CSG.

Upon assignment to USAFE, Sixteenth Air Force's area of responsibility included only the Iberian Peninsula, the Balearic Isles, Morocco, and the Canary Islands. In 1968, impelled by Soviet naval and air buildups in the Mediterranean area, USAFE reorganized its command lines in NATO's Southern Region. Formally designated as the 7217th Air Division and commanded by a brigadier general, The U.S. Logistics Group (TUSLOG) supervised USAFE units in Greece and Turkey. In addition, Seventeenth Air Force initially commanded all USAFE units in Italy and Libya, as well as those in Western Europe's Central Region. After a yearlong phase-in period for the reorganization, USAFE assigned Sixteenth Air Force full command responsibility for units and bases in Spain, Italy, Libya, Greece and Turkey on 1 April 1969. All these countries rested along the strategic west-to-east Mediterranean lines of communication (LOCs).

Although Headquarters TUSLOG became a subordinate organization of Sixteenth Air Force on 23 October 1968, it still retained direct command of the units in Greece and Turkey. These were the 7206th Support Group at Athenai Airport, Greece; the 39th Tactical Group (TACG) at Incirlik AB; the 41st TACG at Cigli AB; the 7250th Support Group at Ankara; and the 7241st Support Squadron at Istanbul. Under a system known as the Turkey cover plan, each of the units serving in country were to be publicly referred to as TUSLOG numbered detachments. For example, the 39th TACG was known as TUSLOG Detachment 10, and the 41st TACG as TUSLOG Det 116. In addition to meeting NATO Sixth Allied Tactical Air Force (SIXATAF) alert commitments at Cigli and Incirlik, TUSLOG provided logistical support to all U.S. Government personnel and agencies in Turkey. The 7206th bore a similar responsibility in Greece.

Having acquired Wheelus AB, Libya, in December 1968, Sixteenth Air Force became USAFE's training range manager in the Mediterranean area. However, 1969 also witnessed a major change in this new mission. Only a few months later, in September 1969, a group of radical young officers overthrew the government of King Idris I of Libya, and they immediately demanded that the United States withdraw its forces from their country. After a rapid drawdown, USAFE discontinued the 7272^{d} Flying Training Wing (FTW) and closed Wheelus on 11 June 1970. This closure led USAFE to examine its base resources in order to find a replacement for Wheelus' training range. Eventually, with Spanish concurrence, USAFE selected Zaragoza for its nearby Bardenas Reales range. Accordingly, USAFE returned Zaragoza AB to main operating base status and activated the 406th Tactical Fighter Training Group on 1 July 1970, and later, upgraded it to wing level on 15 July 1972. Meanwhile, on 1 January 1970, as part of the Project REDCOSTE reductions, USAFE placed Morón AB in standby status, ending the fair-weather deployments of its tactical reconnaissance aircraft to that base. Hence, the 7473d CSG at Morón became a Combat Support Squadron.

In addition to the Zaragoza Weapons Training Site (WTS), USAFE had other ranges in the Sixteenth Air Force area available for use. An early favorite as an alternative to Zaragoza was Decimomannu AB on the island of Sardinia. A detachment of the 401st TFW became the operator of the WTS at Decimomannu by utilizing the Italian Air Force (IAF) Capo Frasco range for Third Air Force and Seventeenth Air Force Weapons Training Detachments (WTDs). However, USAFE found the cost of expanding the base for such operations to be prohibitive, and it effectively closed the WTS in November 1971 with the withdrawal of the last Third Air Force WTD. Meanwhile, WTDs from Third and Seventeenth Air Forces began deploying to Aviano to use the IAF's Maniago range, while the 401st TFW rotational squadron at Incirlik continued training on the Turkish Air Force gunnery range at Konya.

Although the use of Spanish ranges was negotiated separately, the command's dependence on these facilities highlighted the problem of continued availability of Spanish basing. The 1953 agreement ran out in 1968 without the United States and Spain reaching an accord. Then in 1969, the two countries extended the agreement retroactively for a two-year period in order to negotiate an entirely new agreement. This took the form of the Agreement of

Friendship and Cooperation (AFC), signed on 9 August 1970. The AFC was to run for a basic five-year period and could be renewed for another five years if both sides agreed. For use of the bases, which ceased being "joint-use" by completely coming under SAF command, the United States gave Spain credits to buy a wing of F-4Cs in Project PEACE ALPHA and agreed to participate in the modernization of the Spanish air defense system in Project COMBAT GRANDE. The AFC also established a high-level Joint Committee and an operational-level U.S. - Spanish Joint Air Control and Coordination Center (JACCC). Headquarters USAFE activated the American segment of the JACCC on 15 October 1971 and assigned it to Sixteenth Air Force.

At the other end of the Mediterranean, the United States and Turkey signed a new Defense Cooperation Agreement (DCA) on 1 July 1969. This new agreement, which replaced a plethora of former accords, specified that the two countries would negotiate individual implementing agreements for each base or facility required by the United States. The implementing agreement negotiations proved difficult, continuing until the DCA itself was suspended.

Over the years, TUSLOG had been subject to an uncertain organizational future and a target for a seemingly endless series of plans for reorganizations and reduction. Then, on 10 September 1970 after an 11-year existence as a divisional headquarters, HQ TUSLOG was reduced to a detachment of Headquarters Sixteenth Air Force. Interestingly, the rank of its commander was increased from a brigadier general to a major general within the same time frame. Earlier, on 30 June 1970, USAFE inactivated the 41st TACG (TUSLOG Det 116) and turned Cigili AB over to the

TAF as a standby base with operations and maintenance (O&M) funding provided by Headquarters USAF. The 7241st ABG (TUSLOG Det 118) replaced Det 116 as the responsible unit at Izmir on 1 July 1970. Its mission was to maintain war readiness materiel (WRM) at Cigili AB and to support the Izmir area NATO headquarters of SIXATAF and Allied Land Forces Southeast Europe (LANDSOUTHEAST). Both the 39th TACG and the 7241st ABG were assigned directly to Sixteenth Air Force, while TUSLOG's detachment at Istanbul fell victim to Project REDCOSTE cutbacks in force structure and manning.

The same reorganization action also affected Greece as USAFE reassigned the 7206th Support Group from TUSLOG to Sixteenth Air Force on 10 September 1970. Later, the unit redesignated as the 7206th ABG on 1 January 1973, and the Greeks renamed the base Hellenikon AB in February 1976. Also, in 1973, the group acquired a new mission when the U.S. Sixth Fleet determined to "home port" certain components of its forces at Athens. Earlier, the 7206th had been subjected to Project REDCOSTE cuts, but it now became necessary to assign additional manpower authorizations at Athenai to provide emerging support to U.S. Navy elements.

A year after the organizational reductions, the pendulum swung the other way in Turkey, when on 15 October 1971, USAFE upgraded TUSLOG to a wing-level "named" organization under Sixteenth Air Force. The TUSLOG commander again assumed supervisory responsibilities for units in Turkey. Efforts to phase down USAF activities as Ankara continued, and on 30 March 1973, Headquarters USAFE eliminated the 7250th Support

Squadron (TUSLOG Det 30) at Ankara by combining its residual base support functions with the HQ TUSLOG staff.

New Home

The new Spanish/U.S. Defense Cooperation Agreement was ratified by both Spain and the U.S. in 1989, and it mandated the withdrawal of the 401st TFW from Spain by 1992 and of the Sixteenth Air Force headquarters by 1997. Headquarters USAF decided to withdraw both the 401st and Sixteenth Air Force by the earlier date, inactivate Sixteenth Air Force's 406th Tactical Fighter Training Wing, and terminate USAF activities at Zaragoza AB. These events also coincided with the end of the Cold War, which also demanded a reexamination of the roles that NAFs played while Sixteenth Air Force searched for a new home.

The rapid collapse of the Soviet Union and subsequent dismemberment of the Warsaw Pact accelerated the U.S. Congress' desire to reduce the size of and expenditures on military forces. The drawdown in the military began affecting Sixteenth Air Force directly when in January 1990, the Department of Defense (DoD) announced the closure of twelve overseas bases to include Hellenikon AB and Comiso AS. However, with a realignment of communications function from the Air Force Communications Command (AFCC) to other Air Force major commands (MAJCOM), Sixteenth Air Force gained the 1989th Communications Wing at Torrejón AB. Yet later, as part of the effort to reduce costs, USAFE notified the IAF that it would stop operating the weapons training installation at Decimomannu AB by September 1991.

During these significant changes, a new conflict

Major General **Winfield Scott Harpe** (12 January 1937 – 5 December 1988) Commanding General of the 16th Air Force, sits in the cockpit of F-16A block 15 #82-0975 at Torrejón AB on 7 September 1988.

On 5 December 1988, the Block 30D F-16C he was flying on a training flight, AF serial 86-0316, crashed near Chiloeches, in the Spanish province of Guadalajara, which is close to Torrejón Air Base, outside of Madrid during an attempted forced landing after a technical failure while on a routine training mission. The general was killed in the crash. An Air Force spokesman said the general was participating in a training mission, flying in formation with three other planes and was near the end of a 90-minute training flight when he crashed.

erupted in the Middle East that would demand much of Sixteenth Air Force units. On 2 August 1990, Iraq invaded its smaller neighbor Kuwait declaring it a lost province. Five days later, President Bush ordered aircraft and ground troops to defend Saudi Arabia in what was named Operation DESERT SHIELD. Sixteenth Air Force units were some of the first to respond to the call, and several were critical to the movement of forces to the Persian Gulf region. On 29 August 1990, 24 F-16s from the 401st TFW's 614th Tactical Fighter Squadron (TFS) deployed to Doha, Qatar, under the 401st TFW (Provisional). Weeks later, the 614th's sister 612th TFS deployed 20 F-16s to join four of its F-16s already in place at Incirlik AB, where they had been conducting a WTD. These two 401st units would both later fly combat operations during the subsequent Operation DESERT STORM. Incirlik AB itself became a significant site of combat operations when in January 1991 it hosted the Joint Task Force-PROVEN FORCE that conducted the air war over northern Iraq.

In supporting roles, Torrejón, Morón, and Zaragoza all served as major transit points for the thousands of military personnel and a massive tonnage of equipment flowing to bases in the Middle East. These latter bases continued to support the return flow of people and materiel back to the U.S. after the end of combat operations in March 1991, and Incirlik AB continued to be a focal point for missions in Iraq with the follow-on Operation PROVIDE COMFORT.

As the Persian Gulf War grew to a close and the Air Force reconstituted itself after the conflict, plans for the movement of the 401st and Sixteenth Air Force proceeded ahead at a relatively rapid pace. Although a new NATO base was to be built initially at Crotone, Italy, which would serve as both units' new home, the costs involved proved to be prohibitive, especially in the aftermath of the war. As an alternative, USAFE selected Aviano AB to be the temporary home for the 401st and Sixteenth Air Force because it possessed some permanent facilities and represented a cheaper investment at the time. Shorn of its operational fighter squadrons, the 401st was the first to make the transition when it inactivated at Torrejón on 4 May 1992, and stood up the same day at Aviano, assuming the personnel and resources of the 40th Support Wing.

U.S. Mission for Military Assistance to Turkey (JUSMMAT) to economize on joint force expenditures. TUSLOG essentially remained in name only until it was officially inactivated a year later. Another unit, the 406th TFTW at Zaragoza, inactivated in June 1992, and Morón's status reverted to a pre- Gulf War standby base. Other functions and bases in the command appeared to be in danger of imminent closure as well, and there was even discussion at this stage of inactivating Sixteenth Air Force entirely. However, as events in the Middle East continued to simmer and new crises arose in the nearby Balkans, Air Force and NATO leaders recognized the need to retain a

16th AF Headquarter at Torrejón AB

continued command presence in the much-troubled Southern Region.

The beginning of the Expeditionary era

The 401st FW moved from Spain to Aviano AB, Italy, in May 1992 and was re-designated as the 31st FW in April 1994. It has two squadrons of F-16C/Ds. Headquarters, 16th AF moved to Aviano AB in August 1992.

During its time at Aviano AB, Sixteenth Air Force was the operational air force for USAF combat operations in the Balkans, supporting Operation Deny Flight, enforcing the U.N. ordered no-fly zone over Bosnia. Sixteenth Air Force aircraft participated in the raid on the Bosnian-Serb held airfield at Udbina in November 1994. In the fall of 1995, 16th AF supported Operation Deliberate Force, the U.N.-sanctioned/NATO executed attacks on Bosnian-Serb forces. In 1995, 16th AF supported Operation Joint Endeavor, the NATO peacekeeping mission to the former Yugoslavia, through operations in Croatia, Hungary and Bosnia-Herzegovina.

The years 1996 through 1998 saw continued high operations in 16th AF. It was the first Air Force organization to fully employ the Expeditionary Wing concept. The 16th Air and Space Expeditionary Task Force, consisting of the 16th and 31st Air Expeditionary Wings, activated in support of Operation Joint Guardian, and its air component, Operation Deliberate Guard, engaging air power for peace enforcement operations in Bosnia-Herzegovina. The 39th Air & Space Expeditionary Wing activated in support of Operation Northern Watch, engaging air power to enforce the no-fly zone over northern Iraq.

In 2005, Sixteenth Air Force moved to Ramstein AB, Germany to become USAFE's new Warfighting Headquarters. Its mission was to execute aerospace operations through expeditionary force command and control in support of the U.S. European Command and NATO. Supporting this mission, 16th AF planned and executed combat air operations in southern Europe and portions of the Middle East and northern Africa as an air component or joint task force headquarters. It supported approximately 11,000 Air Force and civilian members at two main operating bases, four support bases and other sites in Spain, France, Germany, Italy, Croatia, Kosovo, Bosnia-Herzegovina, Hungary, Macedonia, Greece, Turkey and Israel; and conducted peacetime engagement throughout the region.

On 1 December 2006, the Sixteenth Air Force was inactivated at Ramstein AB and simultaneously reconstituted as the *Sixteenth Air Expeditionary Task Force* at Izmir Air Base, Turkey. It was replaced at Ramstein by the Third Air Force. The 16th AETF was inactivated in April 2008.

On September 18, 2019, *Sixteenth Air Force* (16th AF) will be the designation for a new Information Warfare (IW) *Numbered Air Force* (NAF).

SAC MEMORIAL CHAPEL
Sixteenth Air Force Window

The shield of the Sixteenth Air Force occupies the top portion of the right side of this window. Because the primary mission of the Sixteenth Air Force was support of SAC units on alert or schedule for emergency operations during the first year of its existence, it is placed in the center of the left portion the "**FAMOUS RED TELEPHONE**" at SAC Headquarters – symbol of instant global alert—readiness. Illustrative of the Sixteenth Air Force becoming SAC's first overseas air force is the outline shapes of Iceland and French Morocco in the upper left portion. The portrayal in the bottom left section, superimposed upon the outline Spain, is an abstract of the 480-mile pipeline which bisects that nation especially to fuel SAC aircraft. The radar screen and radarscope, together with the B-47 represented in the lower right portion, illustrate the 4310TH Air Division, which is responsible for monitoring the reflex operations of SAC units in North Africa.

Chapter III

65TH AIR DIVISION

Established as 4th Air Defense Wing on 25 Mar 1943. Activated on 27 Mar 1943. Redesignated 65th Fighter Wing on 24 Jul 1943. The 65th wing and its subordinate units transferred to England in Jun 1943 and began flying combat missions. Subordinate units escorted bombers, flew counter air patrols, and dive-bombing missions. They attacked airdromes, marshalling yards, missile sites, industrial areas, ordnance depots, oil refineries, trains, and highways. During "Big Week", 20-25 Feb 1944, the 65th participated in the assaults against the German Air Force and the German aircraft industry. Its units supported the Allied invasion of Normandy (Jun 1944); the Allied ground troops during the Battle of the Bulge (Dec 1944 Jan 1945); the Allied airborne attack on Holland (Operation Market-Garden, Sep 1944); the defense of the Remagen bridgehead against German air attacks (Mar 1945); and the airborne attack across the Rhine (Mar 1945). As an Air Division, it carried out air defense operations in Iceland 1952-1954. Activated three years later it transferred to Spain, where it cooperated with Spanish Air Force units in the Air Defense Direction Centers (ADDCs). The 65th Air Division directed base construction, and the establishment of off base housing and radar sites. Its fighter squadrons

flew air defense interceptions over Spanish airspace. The 65th also controlled the operations of attached tactical fighter squadrons deployed to Spain for temporary duty. Assigned or attached units of the division participated in numerous exercises with the Spanish Air Defense Command, and in some instances, with the U.S. Sixth Fleet. In Jun 1985, the 65th assumed responsibility for integrating USAFE's electronic combat systems to maximize overall warfighting potential.

Lineage

- Established as 4 Air Defense Wing on 25 Mar 1943.
- Activated on 27 Mar 1943.
- Redesignated 65 Fighter Wing on 24 Jul 1943.
- Inactivated on 21 Nov 1945.
- Redesignated 65 Air Division (Defense) on 17 Apr 1952.
- Organized on 24Apr 1952.
- Discontinued on 8 Mar 1954.
- Activated on 8 Apr1957.
- Discontinued, and inactivated, on 1 Jan 1965.
- Redesignated 65 Air Division and activated on 1 Jun 1985.
- Inactivated on 30 Jun 1991.

Assignments

- Fourth Air Force, 27 Mar 1943.
- Army Service Forces, 6 May 1943.
- Eighth Air Force, 2 Jun 1943.
- VIII Fighter Command, 4 Jun 1943.
- 2nd Bombardment (later, 2nd Air) Division, 15 Sep 1944.

- 3[d] Air Division, 1 Jun-21 Nov 1945.
- Iceland Air Defense Force, 24 Apr 1952-8 Mar 1954.
- Sixteenth Air Force, 8 Apr 1957.
- United States Air Forces in Europe, 1 Jul 1960 - 1 Jan 1965.
- Seventeenth Air Force, 1 Jun 1985 - 30 Jun 1991.

Components

Wings.
52nd Tactical Fighter: 1 Jun 1985-30 Jun 1991.
66th Electronic Combat: 1 Jun 1985-30 Jun 1991.
601st Tactical Control: 1 Jun 1985-31 Jul 1987.

Groups.
4th Fighter: by 31 Oct 1943-c. 31 May 1945.
56th Fighter: by 31 Oct 1943-by 31 May 1945.
78th Fighter: c. 24 Jul 1943-unkn.
355th Fighter: by 31 Oct 1943-by 31 May 1945.
356th Fighter: by 31 Oct 1943-by 31 Aug 1944.
361st Fighter: by 31 Aug 1944-by 31 Jan 1945; by 30 Apr-by 31 May 1945.
479th Fighter: by 31 May 1944-by 31 May 1945.

Squadrons.
1st Fighter Day (later, 1 Tactical Fighter): attached 27 Jun-c. 12 Nov 1958.
82nd Fighter-Interceptor: 1 Apr 1953-8 Mar 1954.
157th Fighter-Interceptor: 23 Nov 1961-17 Jul 1962.
307th Tactical Fighter: attached 13 Mar-c. 31 Jul 1959.
308th Tactical Fighter: attached c. Aug-16 Nov 1959.
334th TacticalFighter: attached 1 Apr-13 Aug 1963.

Base construction early 1950's

First hangars 1950's

336th Tactical Fighter: attached 13 Aug 1963-6 Jan 1964.

430th Tactical Fighter: attached 25 Sep-25 Nov 1961.
431st Fighter-Interceptor: 1 Sep 1958-1 Jul 1960; attached 1 Jul 1960-c. 18 May 1964.
434th Tactical Fighter: attached 18 Mar 1960-unkn; 14 Aug-25 Sep 1961.
435th Tactical Fighter: attached 15 Dec 1960-14 Apr 1961; 6 Aug-l Nov 1962; 2 Apr-18 Jun 1964.
436th Tactical Fighter: attached 1 Nov 1962-3 Apr 1963.
474th Tactical Fighter: attached 15 Nov 1958-14 Mar 1959.
476th Tactical Fighter: attached 16 Nov 1959-18 Mar 1960; 16 Apr-11 Aug 1961; 6 Jan-2 Apr 1964.
497th Fighter-Interceptor: 5 Jul 1958-1 Jul 1960; attached 1 Jul 1960-17 Jun 1964.

Flight.
1 Gunnery and Tow: 17 Nov 1944-29 May 1945.

Stations

Hamilton Field, CA, 27 Mar-6 May 1943.
Debden, England, 4 Jun 1943.
Saffron Walden, England, c. 17 Jun 1943.
Elvedon Hall, England, c. 1 Sep 1945.
Trosten, England, c. 25 Oct-21 Nov 1945.
Keflavik Airport, Iceland, 24 Apr 1952-8 Mar 1954.
Madrid, Spain, 8 Apr 1957.
Torrejón AB, Spain, 1 Oct 1957-1Jan 1965.
Sembach AB, Germany, 1 Jun 1985.
Lindsey AS, Germany, 1 Oct 1987-30 Jun 1991.

Hangar construction early 50s

Construction of the first hangars, 1957

Commanders

Unkn, 27 Mar 1943.
Col Jesse Auton, 10 Apr 1943.
Brig Gen Ross G. Hoyt, 4 Jun 1943.
Brig Gen Jesse Auton, 6 Sep 1943.
Col William L. Curry, 29 Jul 1945-unkn.
1st Lt John J. Brody, 24 Apr 1952.
Col Meredith H. Shade, 10 Oct 1952.
Col Emmett S. Davis, 5 Sep 1953-unkn.
Capt Newell H. Beaty, 8 Apr 1957.
Col Clay Tice Jr., 15 May 1957.
Brig Gen Andrew J. Evans Jr., 1 Jul 1960.
Col Thomas L. Hayes, 25 Sep 1963-1 Jan 1965.
Unkn, 1 Jun-14 Jul 1985.
Maj Gen John C. Scheidt Jr., 15 Jul 1985.
Brig Gen Philip M. Drew, 12 Aug 1986.
Brig Gen John A. Corder, 3 Aug 1987.
Brig Gen Gerald A. Daniel, 22 Apr 1988.
Brig Gen Glenn A. Profitt II, 24 Jan 1989-unk.

Aircraft

P-38, 1944;
P-47, 1943 - 1945;
P-51, 1944 - 1945.
F-94, 1952 - 1954;
F-86, 1953 - 1954.
F-86, 1957 - 1960;
F-100, 1958 - 1961;
F-104, 1959 - 1964;
F-102, 1960 - 1964;
F-105, 1963 - 1964.

Torrejón Air Base, 1963

SPAF and USAF Air Controllers at Torrejón, 1962

CH-53, 1985 - 1987;
EF-111, 1985 - 1991;
F-4, 1985 - 1987;
EC-130, 1987 - 1991;
F-16, 1987 - 1991.

Decorations

Air Force Outstanding Unit Awards:
20 Mar 1961-9 Feb 1962.
15 Apr 1989-14 Apr 1991.

Torrejón Air Base Construction, beginning of the 50s

Torrejón Air Base Spain, 1958

Chapter IV

STRATEGIC AIR COMMAND

Strategic Air Command (**SAC**) was both a *United States Department of Defense* (DoD) Specified Command and a *United States Air Force* (USAF) *Major Command* (MAJCOM), responsible for Cold War command and control of two of the three components of the U.S. military's strategic nuclear strike forces, the so-called "nuclear triad," with

SAC having control of land-based strategic bomber aircraft and *intercontinental ballistic missiles* or ICBMs (the third leg of the triad being submarine-launched ballistic missiles (SLBM) of the U.S. Navy).

SAC also operated all strategic reconnaissance aircraft, all strategic airborne command post aircraft, and all USAF aerial refueling aircraft, to include those in the *Air Force Reserve* (AFRES) and *Air National Guard* (ANG).

However, SAC did not operate the KB-50, WB-50 and WB-47 weather reconnaissance aircraft operated through the mid and late 1960s by the Air Weather Service, nor did SAC operate the HC-130 or MC-130 operations aircraft capable of aerial refueling helicopters that were assigned to Tactical Air Command (TAC), then Military Airlift Command (MAC), and from 1990 onward, those MC-

130 aircraft operated by the *Air Force Special Operations Command* (AFSOC), or any AFRES (now *Air Force Reserve Command* (AFRC)) or ANG tactical aerial refueling aircraft (e.g., HC-130, MC-130) operationally gained by TAC, MAC or AFSOC.

SAC primarily consisted of the *Second Air Force* (2AF), *Eighth Air Force* (8AF) and the *Fifteenth Air Force* (15AF), while SAC headquarters (HQ SAC) included Directorates for Operations & Plans, Intelligence, Command & Control, Maintenance, Training, Communications, and Personnel. At a lower echelon, SAC headquarters divisions included Aircraft Engineering, Missile Concept, and Strategic Communications.

In 1992, as part of an overall post-Cold War reorganization of the U.S. Air Force, SAC was disestablished as both a Specified Command and as a MAJCOM, and its personnel and equipment redistributed among the *Air Combat Command* (ACC), Air Mobility Command (AMC), *Pacific Air Forces* (PACAF), United States Air Forces in Europe (USAFE), and Air Education and Training Command (AETC), while SAC's central headquarters complex at Offutt AFB, Nebraska was concurrently transferred to the newly created *United States Strategic Command* (USSTRATCOM), which was established as a joint Unified Combatant Command to replace SAC's Specified Command role.

Background

In 2009, SAC's previous USAF MAJCOM role was reactivated and redesignated as the Air Force Global Strike Command (AFGSC), with AFGSC eventually acquiring claimancy and control of all USAF bomber aircraft and the USAF strategic ICBM force.

The Strategic Air Forces of the United States during World War II included General Carl Spaatz's European command, *United States Strategic Air Forces in Europe* (USSTAF), consisting of the 8AF and 15AF, and the *United States Strategic Air Forces in the Pacific* (USASTAF) and its *Twentieth Air Force* (20AF).

The U.S. Army Air Forces' first mission in the Strategic Bombing Campaign in the European Theater during World War II included the VIII Bomber Command, which conducted the first European "heavy bomber" attack by the USAAF on 17 August 1942; the Ninth Air Force, which conducted the first Operation Crossbow "No-Ball" missions on 5 December 1943; the Twelfth Air Force; and the Fifteenth Air Force, which executed bombing operations on 2 November 1943 during Operation Pointblank.

The Operation Overlord air plan for the strategic bombing of both Germany and German military forces in continental Europe prior to the 1944 invasion of France used several Air Forces, primarily those of the USAAF and those of the Royal Air Force (RAF), with command of air operations transferring to the Supreme Commander of the Allied Expeditionary Force on 14 April 1944.

Planning to reorganize for a separate and independent postwar U.S. Air Force had begun by the fall of 1945, with the Simpson Board tasked to plan, "*...the reorganization of the Army and the Air Force...*". In January 1946, Generals Eisenhower and Spaatz agreed on an Air Force organization composed of the Strategic Air

B-47 Stratojet at Torrejón Air Base, 1959

SAC 16th AF, 1960

Command, the Air Defense Command, the Tactical Air Command, the Air Transport Command and the supporting Air Technical Service Command, Air Training Command, the Air University, and the Air Force Center.

Strategic Air Command was originally established in the U.S. Army Air Forces on 21 March 1946, acquiring part of the personnel and facilities of the Continental Air Forces (CAF), the World War II command tasked with the air defense of the continental United States (CONUS). At the time, CAF headquarters was located at Bolling Field (later Bolling AFB) in the District of Columbia and SAC assumed occupancy of its headquarters facilities until relocating SAC headquarters (HQ SAC) to nearby Andrews Field (later Andrews AFB), Maryland as a tenant activity until assuming control of Andrews Field in October 1946.

SAC initially totaled 37,000 USAAF personnel. In addition to Bolling Field and, seven months later, Andrews Field, SAC also assumed responsibility for:

- Roswell AAF, New Mexico (later renamed Roswell AFB, then Walker AFB), then home of the USAAF's sole nuclear-capable bomb wing, and
- Smoky Hill AAF, Kansas (later renamed Smoky Hill AFB, then Schilling AFB)
- SAC also had seven additional CAF bases transferred on 21 March 1946 which remained in SAC through the 1947 establishment of the U.S. Air Force as an independent service. Those installations included:
- Castle Field, California (later Castle Air Force Base)
- Clovis AAF, New Mexico (later Cannon Air Force Base)
- Fort Worth AAF, Texas (later Carswell Air Force Base)

B-47 over Segovia

- Davis-Monthan Field, Arizona (later Davis-Monthan Air Force Base)
- Rapid City AAF, South Dakota (later Ellsworth Air Force Base)
- MacDill Field, Florida (later MacDill Air Force Base)
- Mountain Home AAF, Idaho (later Mountain Home Air Force Base)

On 31 March 1946, the following additional installation was also assigned to SAC:

- Kirtland Field, New Mexico (later Kirtland Air Force Base)

Under the first SAC Commander in Chief, General George C. Kenney, initial units reporting to the Strategic Air Command headquarters on 21 March 1946 included the Second Air Force, the IX Troop Carrier Command and the 73rd Air Division.

Fifteenth Air Force was assigned to SAC on 31 March (15th AF's 263rd Army Air Force Base Unit—with SAC's radar detachments—transferred the same date directly under HQ SAC), while the IX Troop Carrier Command was inactivated the same date and its assets redistributed within SAC.

With postwar demobilization still underway, eight of the ten assigned bomb groups were inactivated before the Eighth Air Force was assigned to SAC on 7 June 1946.

Despite the pressures of demobilization, SAC continued the training and evaluation of bomber crews and units still on active duty in the postwar Army Air Forces.

B-47 over Zaragoza

Radar Bomb Scoring became the preferred method of evaluating bomber crews, with the last of 888 simulated bomb runs scored against a bombing site near San Diego, California during 1946, subsequently increasing to 2,449 bomb runs by 1947. In the wake of the successful employment of air-dropped nuclear weapons against Hiroshima and Nagasaki to effectively end World War II, SAC became the focus of the nation's nuclear strike capability, to the extent that Joint Chiefs of Staff (JCS) Publication 1259/27 on 12 December 1946 identified that, "*...the 'air atomic' strategic air force should only come under the orders of the JCS.*"

In addition to the strategic bombing mission, SAC also devoted significant resources to aerial reconnaissance. In 1946, SAC's reconnaissance aircraft inventory consisted of F-2 photo variants of the C-45 Expeditor support aircraft, but by 1947 SAC had acquired an F-9C squadron consisting of twelve photo-reconnaissance variants of the B-17G Flying Fortress. An F-13 squadron, the F-13 later re-designated as the RB-29 Superfortress, was also established. SAC conducted routine aerial reconnaissance missions near the Soviet borders or near the 12-mile international waters limit, although some missions penetrated Soviet airspace. The flight profiles of these missions—above 30,000 feet and in excess of 300 knots—made interception by Soviet air forces difficult until the Soviet's 1948 introduction of the MiG-15 jet fighter. Project Nanook, the Cold War's first Top Secret reconnaissance effort, used the first RB-29 missions for mapping and visual reconnaissance in the Arctic and along the northern Soviet coast. Later missions were

B-58 HUSTLER in Torrejón AB, 1958

RB-47E over Spain

Project LEOPARD along the Chukchi Peninsula, followed by Projects RICKRACK, STONEWORK, and COVERALLS.

In 1946, the US possessed only nine atomic bombs and twenty-seven B-29s capable at any one time of delivering them. Furthermore, it was later determined that an attack by the 509th Composite Bomb Group during the 1947 to 1948 time frame would have required at least five to six days just to transfer custody of the bombs from United States Atomic Energy Commission (AEC) sites to SAC and deploy the aircraft and weapons to forward operating bases before launching nuclear strikes.

Unfortunately, postwar budget and personnel cuts had had an insidious effect on SAC as its Deputy Commander, Major General Clements McMullen, implemented mandated force reductions. This continued to wear down SAC as a command and morale plummeted. As a result, by the end of 1947, only two of SAC's eleven groups were combat ready. After the 1948 Bikini Atoll nuclear tests, the "Half Moon" Joint Emergency War Plan developed in May 1948 proposed dropping 50 atomic bombs on twenty Soviet cities, with President Harry S. Truman approving "Half Moon" during the June 1948 Berlin Blockade, (Truman sent B-29s to Europe in July). SAC also ordered special ELINT RB-29s to detect improved Soviet radars and, in cooperation with the 51st Air Force Base Unit, SAC also monitored radioactive fallout from Soviet atomic testing on Novaya Zemlya. In terms of overall Air Force basing and infrastructure, SAC continued to acquire an ever-increasing share of USAF infrastructure and the USAF associated budget. In 1947, before the USAF was established as an independent service, construction commenced on Limestone AAF, Maine (later renamed

Torrejón Air Base Spain, 1961

Aircraft marshalling at Torrejón AB, 1963

Loring AFB), a new SAC installation specifically designed to accommodate the B-36 Peacemaker. Fort Dix AAF, New Jersey (later McGuire AFB); Spokane AAF, Washington (later Fairchild AFB); and Wendover Field, Utah (later Wendover AFB) were also transferred to SAC between 30 April and 1 September 1947. Following establishment of the USAF as a separate service, SAC bases in the United States consisted of:

- Castle Air Force Base, California
- Patrick Air Force Base, Florida
- Cannon Air Force Base, New Mexico
- Carswell Air Force Base, Texas
- Davis-Monthan Air Force Base, Arizona
- Ellsworth Air Force Base, South Dakota
- MacDill Air Force Base, Florida
- Mountain Home Air Force Base, Idaho
- Kirtland Air Force Base, New Mexico
- Loring Air Force Base, Maine
- McGuire Air Force Base, New Jersey
- Fairchild Air Force Base, Washington
- Wendover Air Force Base, Utah
- Wendover Air Force Base, Utah

Korean War

In July 1950, in response to combat operations on the Korean peninsula, SAC dispatched ten nuclear-capable bombers to Guam and deployed four B-29 bomber wings in Korea for tactical operations, although this action caused SAC commander Lemay to comment, *"...too many splinters were being whittled off the [deterrence] stick".*

B-47'S Reflex refueling on their way to Torrejón, 1958

View of the runway with B-47's Torrejón AB

Initial SAC B-29 successes against North Korea in the summer of 1950 were countered by subsequent Soviet MiG-15 fighter-interceptors, and SAC's 27th Fighter Escort Wing began escorting the bombers with F–84 Thunderjets. Ground-directed bombing (GDB) was subsequently used for close air support (CAS) missions after three SAC radar bomb scoring (RBS) squadron detachments (Dets C, K, & N) arrived at Pusan in September 1950. In 1951, SAC "began to eliminate its combat groups", transferring medium bombardment groups "to Far East Air Forces (FEAF) Bomber Command for combat." In 1951, LeMay convinced the Air Staff to allow SAC to approve nuclear targets, and he continued refusing to submit war plans for JCS review, which the JCS eventually came to accept (of 20,000 candidates in 1960, SAC designated 3,560 as bombing targets—mostly Soviet air defense: airfields and suspected missile sites.)

Although experimented with prior to World War II, SAC refined aerial refueling to a fine art. SAC's in-flight refueling mission began in July 1952 when its 31st Fighter-Escort Wing refueled sixty F-84G Thunderjets from Turner AFB, Georgia to Travis AFB, California non-stop with fuel from twenty-four KB-29P Superfortresses modified into aerial tankers. Exercise FOX PETER ONE followed with 31st FEW fighters being refueled Hickam AFB in route to Hawaii

On 15 March 1953, a 38th Strategic Reconnaissance Squadron RB-50 returned fire on a Soviet MiG-15, while a 343^{d} Strategic Reconnaissance Squadron RB-50 was shot down over the Sea of Japan 2 days after the Korean Armistice, while on 7 November 1954, an RB-29 was shot

B-47's Torrejón Air Base Flight Line, 1959

SAC Reflex Crew E72 at Torrejón, 1962. Left to Right, **Bill Stambaugh** NavBombardier, **Bob Bradshaw** co-pilot, **Jack Nelson**, Pilot

down near Hokkaido Island in northern Japan. By the time of 27 July 1953 Korean War cease-fire, SAC B-29s had flown over 21,000 sorties and dropped nearly 167,000 tons of bombs, with thirty-four B-29s lost in combat and forty-eight B-29s were lost to damage or crashes.

The Cold War and massive retaliation

SAC's first jet strategic bomber was the swept-wing B-47 medium bomber, which first entered service in 1951 and became operational within SAC in 1953. The B-47 was a component of the October 1953 New Look strategy, which articulated, in part, that: "*...to minimize the threat...the major purpose of air defense was not to shoot down enemy bombers-it was to allow SAC...to get into the air* [--and] *not be destroyed on the ground* [--to allow] *massive retaliation.*".

Concern of a bomber gap grew after the 1955 Soviet Aviation Day and the Soviets rejected the "Open Skies" Treaty proposed at the Geneva Summit on 21 July 1955. US bomber strength peaked with "over 2,500 bombers" after production "of over 2,000 B-47s and almost 750 B-52s" (circa 1956, 50% of SAC aircraft & 80% of SAC bombers were B-47s).

In an effort to concurrently enhance it reconnaissance capabilities, SAC also received several RB-57D Canberra aircraft in April 1956, with the aircraft initially based at Turner AFB, Georgia. In 1957, these aircraft were forward deployed to Rhein-Main Air Base, West Germany, in order to conduct reconnaissance missions along the borders of the Soviet Union and other Warsaw Pact nations. However, an unintended

Operation Persian Rug 4136th Wing B-52H crew, Torrejón AB (11 Jan 1962)

USAF B-52 Stratofortress crew at Torrejón Air Base, 1962

consequence of this deployment was that Hawker Hunter fighters of the Royal Air Force stationed in the United Kingdom and in continental Europe often intercepted these classified RB-57 missions as they returned to Rhein-Main AB from over the Baltic.

Since it was designed as a medium bomber, SAC's B-47 Stratojet traded speed for range. Because of this shorter range, and in order to better enable the B-47 fleet to reach its target sets in the Soviet Union, SAC routinely deployed its US-based B-47 wings to overseas forward operating bases in North Africa, Spain and Turkey. This program, in effect from 1957 to 1966, was known as "Reflex" with Sixteenth Air Force (16AF), a SAC numbered air force permanently stationed in Europe, having tactical and administrative control of the forward deployed aircraft and units.

Beginning in 1955, SAC also moved a portion of its bomber and aerial refueling aircraft to a 24-hour alert status, either on the ground or airborne. By 1960, fully one third of SAC's bombers and aerial refueling aircraft were on 24-hour alert, with those crews and aircraft not already airborne ready to take off from designated alert sites at their respective bases within fifteen minutes. Bomber aircraft on ground alert were armed with nuclear weapons while aerial tanker aircraft were sufficiently fueled to provide maximum combat fuel offload to the bombers. Concurrent with this increased alert posture and in order to better hone strategic bombing skillsets, the 1955 SAC Bombing and Navigation Competition was characterized by radar bomb scoring (RBS) runs on Amarillo, Denver, Salt Lake City, Kansas City, San Antonio] and Phoenix and the1957 competition

Boeing B-52, Torrejón Air Base, 1962

From Okinawa to Torrejón, 1962

(nicknamed "Operation Longshot") had three targets: Atlanta, Kansas City, and St. Louis. This use of RBS with simulated target areas utilizing mobile and fixed bomb scoring sites adjacent to major cities, industrial areas, military installations and dedicated bombing ranges throughout the United States. This format would continue through successive SAC Bombing and Navigation Competitions through the remainder of the 1950s, 1960s, 1970s and 1980s. Commencing in the late 1950s, in addition to representation from every SAC wing with a bombing and/or air refueling mission, later SAC competitions would also include participating bomber and aerial refueling units from the Royal Air Force's Bomber Command and (after 30 April 1968) its successor, RAF Strike Command.

SAC´s in Vietnam

After the Secretary of Defense rejected LeMay's November 1964 proposal for a "*...strategic air campaign against 94 targets in North Vietnam...*", thirty SAC B-52Fs were deployed to Andersen AFB, Guam on 17 February 1965, representing the first increment of SAC aircraft forward deployed for the Vietnam War. The following month, in March 1965, the Strategic Air Command Advanced Echelon (SACADVON) was established as a "*...liaison unit for CINCSAC* [was] *located at MACV Headquarters to assist with the B-52 effort.*".

On 23 May 1965, SAC B-52Fs began unarmed missions for radar mapping "...and later to test bombing with the assistance of ground homing beacons...". SAC began saturation bombing on 18 June 1965 (8000 tons per

Alert Strip

Special Edition

Depósito Legal M. 10875 - 1961

The ALERT STRIP is an unofficial newspaper published weekly in the interests of personnel at Torrejon Air Base of the Strategic Air Command. It is published by Guidepost Publications, a private firm, in no way connected with the Department of the Air Force. Opinions expressed by publishers and writers are their own and are not to be considered an official expression by the Department of the Air Force. The appearance of advertisements in this publication does not constitute an endorsement by the Department of the Air Force of the products or services advertised.

Vol. V — Torrejon de Ardoz, January 19, 1962 — No. 14

Far out in the Pacific one day last week Major Clyde P. Evely, a large, slow speaking 39 year old Air Force bomber pilot from Petersburg, Va., led his seven man crew to a waiting B-52H Stratofortress bomber parked on the runway at Kadena Air Base, Okinawa. Minutes later when the huge bomber thundered skyward above the blue-green waters of the China Sea the crack eight-man crew from Fifteenth Air Force's 4136th Strategic Wing at Minot AFB, N. D. settled back and pointed the nose of the Stratofortress toward 11 new non-stop distance and course-speed records.

Preparation for the flight of the B-52H, known to Strategic Air Command personnel as a Missile Platform Bomber, set off detailed and around-the-clock activities for Air Force members across half the world and all along the modified great circle route the bomber would follow. The planned 12,519 mile course of the B-52 carried it over check points at Tokyo, Japan; Seattle, Washington; Fort Worth, Texas; Washington D. C.; Lajes, Azores; Madrid, Spain, finally terminated here at Torrejon Air Base.

When the plane, named «Peace Persuader» by the crew, touched down on the Torrejon runway 21 hours and 52 minutes after takeoff from Okinawa a swarm of spectators, newsmen, and military officials were on hand to greet and congratulate the crew on their achievement. Mingled with the music of the Sixteenth Air Force band the screaming engines of the bomber pulled it into place on the parking ramp and Major Evely cut the power on the eight turbofan jet engines to erase all doubt from world opinion concerning the intercontinental capabilities of the Strategic Air Command.

Even as the crew members were lowering themselves from the cavernous fuselage of the bomber Major General David Wade, commander of SAC's 16th Air Force with headquarters at Torrejon Air Base, was standing by to present each crewman with the Distinguished Flying Cross and a handsome engraved plaque commemorating the flight. His congratulations to the crew complimented those messages sent by General Thomas S. Power, SAC Commander-in-chief, and Lt. Gen. Archie J. Old, Jr., Commander of the Fifteenth Air Force. All messages pointed up the importance of proof that the flight furnished regarding SAC aircraft capability in reaching target destinations in any area of the globe.

Given the name «Persian Rug» the non-stop, non-refueled, globe-spanning flight set the following Federation Aeronautique Internationale records: World's distance for all types of aircraft without refueling; World's class «C» distance for jet aircraft without refueling (this record was formely held by General William S. Eubank and crew in a KC-135 at 10,229.3 miles from Tokyo to Lajes in 1958). The remaining nine records are FIA course-speed records; from Tokyo to Seattle to Fort

month in 1966) and conducted Operation Arc Light missions from 1965 until the end of hostilities involving U.S. forces in 1973

On 18 March 1969, along the South Vietnamese border, SAC first bombed Cambodia (Operation Menu through 26 May 1970 was controlled by Skyspot). On 17 February 1970, SAC conducted the first "GOOD LOOK" bombing of Laos at the Plaine des Jarres after B-52 photo recon missions (GOOD LOOK ALPHA in August 1969 and GOOD LOOK BRAVO c. 15 January 1970) and the observations of a Skyspot installation in Thailand. SAC transferred "...HQ 8th AF...to Andersen AFB, Guam on 1 April 1970 to oversee B-52D/G operations and to complement SACADVON". 8th AF took over from Third Air Division the generation of "frag" orders based on daily strike requests and amendments from COMUSMACV.

In 1970, SAC deployed the LGM-30G Minuteman III ICBM with multiple independently targetable reentry vehicle or MIRVs, for striking 3 targets, while concurrently retiring the B-58 Hustler supersonic bomber.

1972 saw the commencement of Operation Linebacker II, a combined Seventh Air Force and U.S. Navy Task Force 77 aerial bombing campaign, conducted against targets in North Vietnam during the final period of US involvement in the Vietnam War. Linebacker II was conducted from 18 December to 29 December 1972, leading to several informal names such as "The December Raids" and "The Christmas Bombings." Unlike the previous Operation Rolling Thunder and Operation Linebacker interdiction operations, Linebacker II, would be a "maximum effort" bombing campaign to destroy major target complexes in the Hanoi and Haiphong areas which could only be accomplished by SAC B-52D/Gs. It saw the largest heavy bomber strikes launched by the U.S. Air Force since the end of World War II. Linebacker II was a modified extension of the Operation Linebacker bombings conducted from May to October 1972, with the emphasis of the new campaign shifted to attacks by B-52 Stratofortress heavy bombers rather than smaller tactical fighter aircraft. During Linebacker II, a total of 741 B-52D/G sorties were dispatched from bases in Thailand and Guam to bomb North Vietnam and 729 completed their missions Overall SAC losses during Linebacker II numbered fifteen B-52s. The U.S. government claimed that the operation had succeeded in forcing North Vietnam's Politburo to return to the negotiating table, with the Paris Peace Accords signed shortly after the operation.

By early 1973, offensive SAC air operations in Southeast Asia ceased and numerous SAC aircrew men who had been shot down and captured as prisoners of war by North Vietnam were repatriated to the United States.

End of the Cold War and Operation Desert Storm

SAC reorganization at the end of the Cold War began as early as 1988 when the Carlucci Commission planned the closure of:

- Mather Air Force Base, California, an ATC undergraduate navigator training (UNT) base which hosted a tenant SAC B-52G / KC-135E bomb wing and a SAC-gained AFRES KC-135A air refueling group; and

- Pease Air Force Base, New Hampshire, a SAC base with an FB-111A and KC-135E bomb wing and a SAC-gained ANG KC-135A air refueling wing.

The closures were the beginning of a post-Cold War process that would later become known as Base Realignment and Closure or BRAC. Although Mather AFB's navigator training mission would relocate to Randolph AFB, Texas, the Mather bomber/tanker wing would inactivate and the AFRES tanker group would relocate to nearby McClellan AFB, relocating again four years later to Beale AFB when another BRAC process would close McClellan AFB.

Concurrently, the Pease AFB bomber/tanker wing would lose its FB-111 aircraft and transfer to Whiteman AFB, Missouri in preparation for transition to the B-2 Spirit while a portion of Pease would be transferred to the New Hampshire Air National Guard for its ANG air refueling wing and be renamed Pease Air National Guard Base.

Additional closures and divestments of SAC bases would continue throughout the late 1980s and early 1990s, accelerating even more so as a result the START I Treaty's mandated elimination of both the entire B-52G fleet and the inactivation of all Minuteman II and Peacekeeper ICBMs, as well as the 1992 reorganization of the Air Force that disestablished SAC and dispersed its assets to other new or existing MAJCOMs, primarily ACC and AMC. In addition to closures of Mather AFB and Pease AFB, this would eventually include the following subsequent closure and realignment actions, primarily due to BRAC:

- Altus AFB (tenant SAC presence disestablished and transferred to AMC, later AETC)
- Barksdale AFB (transferred to ACC, now AFGSC)
- Beale AFB (transferred to ACC)
- Carswell AFB (transferred to USN as NAS JRB Fort Worth per BRAC)
- Castle AFB (closed by BRAC)
- Dyess AFB (transferred to ACC, now AFGSC)
- Eaker AFB (closed by BRAC)
- Ellsworth AFB (transferred to ACC, now AFGSC)
- Fairchild AFB (transferred to AMC)
- F. E. Warren AFB (transferred to ACC, then AFSPC, now AFGSC)
- Grand Forks AFB (transferred to AMC, now ACC)
- Griffiss AFB (closed by BRAC)
- Grissom AFB (transferred to AFRC as Grissom ARB)
- K. I. Sawyer AFB (closed by BRAC)
- Loring AFB (closed by BRAC)
- Malmstrom AFB (transferred to AMC, then AFSPC, now AFGSC)
- March AFB (transferred to AFRC as March ARB per BRAC)
- McConnell AFB (transferred to AMC)
- Minot AFB (transferred to ACC, now AFGSC)
- Offutt AFB (transferred to ACC)
- Plattsburgh AFB (closed by BRAC)
- Robins AFB (tenant Regular AF SAC presence disestablished; base remains an AFMC installation)
- Seymour Johnson AFB (TAC base transferred to ACC; tenant SAC presence disestablished, and SAC-gained tenant AF Reserve presence transferred to AFRC, now gained by AMC)

- Whiteman AFB (transferred to ACC, now AFGSC)
- Wurtsmith AFB (closed by BRAC).

On 1 July 1989, the 1st Combat Evaluation Group reporting directly to SAC headquarters was split with most HQ 1CEVG organizations transferring to SAC HQ (e.g., the Command Instrument Flight Division) and RBS personnel, equipment, and radar stations becoming the 1st Electronic Combat Range Group. Airborne NEACP alerts ended in 1990 and during 1991's Operation Desert Storm to liberate Kuwait from Iraqi invasion and occupation, SAC bomber, tanker and reconnaissance aircraft flew operations (e.g., B-52s with conventional bombs and conventional warhead AGM-86 ALCMs) near Iraq from bases in Great Britain, Turkey, Spain, Cyprus, Diego Garcia, Saudi Arabia, and the United Arab Emirates.

Following Operation Desert Storm, the dissolution of the Soviet Union and the de facto end of the Cold War, President George H. W. Bush and Secretary of Defense Dick Cheney directed SAC to take all bomber and refueling aircraft and Minuteman II ICBM's off of continuous nuclear alert on 27 September 1991 and placing said aircraft on quick reaction ground alert.

The 31 May 1992 major reorganization of the USAF organizational structure subsequently disestablished SAC, moving its bomber, reconnaissance and aerial command post aircraft and all SAC ICBMs, along with all Tactical Air Command aircraft, to the newly established Air Combat Command (ACC). The newly established Air Mobility Command (AMC) inherited most of SAC's KC-135 Stratotanker aircraft and the entire KC-10 Extender aerial refueling tanker force, while some KC-135s were reassigned directly to USAFE and PACAF, with one additional air refueling wing assigned to the Air Education and Training Command (AETC) as the KC-135 formal training unit.

Land-based ICBMs were later transferred from ACC to Air Force Space Command (AFSPC), while manned bombers remained in ACC. USAF nuclear forces in ACC and AFSPC were then combined with the United States Navy's Fleet Ballistic Missile submarine forces to form the United States Strategic Command (USSTRATCOM), which took over the SAC Headquarters complex at Offutt AFB.

In 2009, the entire land-based USAF ICBM force and that portion of the USAF manned bomber force that was still nuclear-capable, e.g., the B-2 Spirit and B-52 Stratofortress, was transferred to the newly established Air Force Global Strike Command (AFGSC), while the B-1 Lancer conventional bomber force remained in ACC. In 2015, these B-1 units were also transferred to Air Force Global Strike Command, which assumed responsibility for all current and future USAF bomber forces.

Components

- Second Air Force: 21 Mar 1946 (from CAF) - 30 Mar 1946; 1 Nov 1949 - 1 Jan 1975
- Eighth Air Force: 7 Jun 1946 - 1 Jun 1992
- Fifteenth Air Force: 31 Mar 1946 - 1 Jun 1992
- Sixteenth Air Force: 1 Jul 1957 - 15 Apr 1966
- IX Troop Carrier Command: 21 Mar 1946 (from CAF) - 31 Mar 1946

Air Divisions

- 1st Air Division (later, 1st Missile Division; 1 Strategic Aerospace Division): 15 Apr 1955 – 20 May 1956; 1 Jan 1958 - 1 Sep 1988
- 3d Air Division: 18 Jun 1954 - 1 Apr 1970; 1 Jan 1975 - 31 Jan 1982
- 5th Air Division: 14 Jan 1951 - 1 Jul 1957
- 7th Air Division: 20 Mar 1951 - 30 Jun 1965; 1 Jul 1978 - 31 Jan 1982
- 21st Air Division: 16 Feb 1951 - 8 Apr 1952; 8 Apr - 16 Jul 1952
- 42nd Air Division: 2 Mar 1951 - 8 Jan 1958; 15 Jul 1959 - 9 Jul 1991
- 58th Air Division: 1 Mar - 16 Oct 1948
- 311th Air Division: 31 Mar 1947 - 1 Nov 1949.

Members of the USAF in front of a B-47 in Torrejón, 1962

Chapter V

98TH STRATEGIC WING

The Nevada Test and Training Range (NTTR) is a United States Air Force unit assigned to the United States Air Force Warfare Center of Air Combat Command. The unit is stationed at Nellis Air Force Base, Nevada as a tenant unit.

The NTTR controls and operates the Nevada Test and Training Range (NTTR). The commander coordinates prioritize and is the approval authority for activities involving other governmental agencies, departments and commercial activities on the NTTR. The NTTR integrates and provides support for test and training programs that have a direct effect on the war-fighting capabilities of the combat air forces.

The history of the NTTR can be traced to its predecessor, the 98th Bombardment Group, a B-24 Liberator heavy bomber group that fought in North Africa and Italy during World War II. The group was last assigned to the range as the 98th Operations Group in 2011 and its history and honors have been temporarily been bestowed on the range. Two of the group's members, Colonel John R. (Killer) Kane and First Lieutenant Donald Pucket were awarded the Medal of Honor for their actions in combat. The group flew a total of 417 missions and earning a total of 15 battle streamers as well as two Distinguished Unit Citations.

During the early years of the Cold War, the 98th Bombardment Wing (BW), Very Heavy was formed in 1947 and assigned to Strategic Air Command. Further redesignations followed as the wing mission changed, including the 98th Strategic Aerospace Wing when it added intercontinental ballistic missiles to its bomber force in 1964, and later the 98th Strategic Wing when it moved to Spain to control deployed Strategic Air Command (SAC) assets in 1966. The 98th Strategic Wing was inactivated on 31 December 1976 with the phaseout of SAC operations at Torrejón AB, Spain and its functions transferred to the 306th Strategic Wing at Ramstein AB, West Germany.

Cold War

The wing remained at Yokota Air Base, Japan in combat-ready status for another year. Meanwhile, wing components not deployed in Japan moved to newly reopened Lincoln AFB, Nebraska to supervise construction in preparation for movement there of the deployed wing components. The wing disposed of its B-29s at the "boneyard" at Davis-Monthan AFB, Arizona. In July 1954, wing components concentrated at the wing's new base, but in October, the 98th gave up its host responsibilities at Lincoln to the 818th Air Division. Air refueling operations were already underway by then. The wing's squadrons began receiving new Boeing B-47E Stratojet swept-wing medium bombers in January 1955, capable of flying at high subsonic speeds and primarily designed for penetrating the airspace of the Soviet Union. At this point the wing began an intensive training program to convert to combat ready status as soon as possible. This was achieved in April 1955.

During next decade, the wing participated in Strategic Air Command's worldwide bombardment training and air refueling commitments. The wing deployed to RAF Lakenheath, England from 11 November 1955 to 29 January 1956. Starting in 1960, the wing maintained B-47s on ground alert 24 hours a day From January 1964 to April 1965, the wing also controlled an SM-65 Atlas intercontinental ballistic missile (ICBM) squadron and was redesignated as the 98th Strategic Aerospace Wing. In the early 1960s, the B-47 was considered to be reaching obsolescence, and was being phased out of SAC's strategic arsenal. Beginning in 1964, the wing began sending its aircraft to Davis-Monthan AFB. Lincoln AFB was closed, and the wing inactivated in 1966.

European Mission

The wing was inactivated on 25 June 1966 at Lincoln AFB, but activated the same day at Torrejón Air Base, Spain replacing the 3970th Strategic Wing (SW). The 3970th SW had been established on 1 July 1957 at Torrejón as the 3970th Air Base Group to support B-47 and KC-135 elements from SAC CONUS-based units deployed to Europe as part of REFLEX deployments and provide a refueling mission to USAFE tactical fighters Until 1 April 1966, when SAC transferred Torrejón to USAFE, the 3970th also acted as the host base organization for all USAF units at Torrejón. The group was assigned seven support squadrons and a hospital to carry out its mission. It was redesignated the 3970th Combat Support Group on 1 June 1959 and upgraded to wing status on 1 February 1964.

In 1966, SAC received authority from Headquarters USAF to discontinue the 3970th SW (a MAJCON wing) and activate an AFCON wing which could continue the lineage and history of a combat wing. On 5 June 1966, the 3970th SW was replaced by the 98th Strategic Wing, which assumed the personnel, equipment, and mission of the 3970th Strategic Wing. For the next decade, the 98th had no tactical aircraft components assigned to it, but rather used attached Boeing KC-135 Stratotankers and crews furnished by other SAC wings to provide air refueling support for the operational, alert exercise commitment of SAC, Tactical Air Command, United States Air Forces Europe and NATO. These aircraft were deployed on temporary duty as the Spanish Tanker Task Force. The wing's operational area included the Eastern Atlantic Ocean, most of Europe, North Africa and the Middle East. The Wing maintained a detachment at RAF Upper Heyford (relocated to RAF Mildenhall in April 1970) supporting RC-135 Reconnaissance Aircraft, and supporting KC-135 Tankers deployed from the Spanish Tanker Task Force. In October 1976, the 306th Strategic Wing, based at Ramstein AB, West Germany assumed this support task and the 98th phased down at Torrejón and was inactivated 31 December 1976.

Stations

- Spokane AAF (later, Spokane AFB; Fairchild AFB), Washington, 10 November 1947 - 15 August 1953
- Yokota AB, Japan, 15 August 1953 - 25 July 1954
- Lincoln AFB, Nebraska, 25 July 1954 - 25 June 1966
- Torrejón AB, Spain, 25 June 1966 - 31 December 1976
- Nellis AFB, Nevada, 29 October 2001 - present.

Chapter VI

497TH FIGHTER INTERCEPTOR SQUADRON

Geiger Field was born on March 11, 1941, when the Department of Defense purchased Sunset Field, southwest of Spokane, WA. The 17th Bombardment Wing, 2nd Bomber Command planned to facilitate training on WWII B-17 and C-47 crews. The name was changed to Geiger Field in honor of Major George Geiger, an Army aviation pioneer.

The first squadron was redeployed to Texas. Many B-17 Bomb Groups and squadrons transferred in and out of Geiger during WWII.

On August 3, 1942, the 922nd Engineer Aviation Regiment was activated at Geiger Field.

In 1944, Geiger Field was completely devoted to training U.S. Army Air Force aviation engineers. Very few transient aircraft flew into Geiger at that time. The aviation engineers were responsible for building air strips, roads, dams and bridges in war zones all over the world.

The 445th FIS was born on the 20th of March in 1953 at Geiger Field. In July, the first F-86D aircraft were assigned. The pilots and airmen were relatively

F-86D Torrejón Air Base 1958

F-86D Torrejón Air Base early 1950'S

inexperienced and the maintenance crew small. Within eighteen months, this group became the finest combat unit in the Western Air Defense Force.

The highpoint in July 1954 was "Operation Checkpoint," a joint SAC-ADC exercise that extended for 3 days. With sunny days and early takeoffs, the pilot's proficiency increased rapidly, and aircraft maintenance became the best in ADC.

In September of 1954, the 445th FIS was named tops in Western Air Defense, and led in hours flows, 810:30 per U.E., aircraft, scramble to airborne and turnaround time.

On 20 November, rocketry training began at Yuma County Airport. When the smoke had cleared, every important Air Defense Command record in FHRT Air Rocketry had been broken.

In March of 1955, the 445th FIS became the first squadron in the 9th Air Division and the second in the Air Defense Command to fly over a thousand hours (1007:45). Outstanding maintenance was a key factor.

In July, the W.A.D.F. Shoot Off was staged at Yuma County Airport. The 445th FIS, once again, took, the 9th Air Division Rocketry trophy.

On July 2, Geiger Field Base Commander, Col. Willcox, presented the 445th FIS with its first Flying Safety plaque. 2,750 hours flown without an accident.

On 17 July 1955, Lt. Colonel Squire T. O'Connor was reassigned to Air Command and Staff School at Maxwell

F-86D at Torrejón Flight Line early 1950'S

F-86D Torrejón Air Base early 1950'S

AFB, Alabama.

The new squadron commander was Lt. Colonel Warren A. Bennett from the 518th FIS, George AFB, CA. He had been assigned as Executive Officer at George.

On February 18, 1953, the 497th FBS was reactivated as a fighter interceptor squadron assigned to the 503rd Air Defense Group based at Portland International Airport in Oregon. The 497th FIX initially flew F-94A Starfires until the spring of 1954, when the F-94A's were replaced with the F-89D.

In August, "Project Arrow" replaced the 445th FIS with the 497th FIS that was moved up from Portland. The 445th FIS was transferred, on paper only, to Oscoda, MI in CADF. The 498th FIS sister squadron, was also activated at Geiger Field in August of 1955. One of the 497th FIS key assignments was to protect the 498th.

The first accident free year was achieved on October 9, 1955, earning a second Flying Safety award. At years end, the Western Air Defense Force honored the 497th FIS with its Ground Safety award for the period.

In February 1956, the squadron made its second deployment to the Yuma desert. The result surpassed the '54 competition. The Air Force record of 225 hits was equaled and all other existing rocketry records were broken.

The 3rd consecutive Flying Safety award was achieved on the 9th of April with 14,005 hours. The flying safety record continued 23 months for a total of 17,217

NORTH AMERICAN F-86D "SABRE DOG"
497TH Fighter Interceptor Squadron (FIS)
TORREJÓN AIR BASE, MADRID (SPAIN) 1959.

hours. A minor accident in September, caused by material failure, ended the streak. This achievement was the result of the outstanding teamwork of the men of the 497th FIS.

Torrejón AB, Spain, opened on June 1957. The 497th FIS was chosen to deploy to Torrejón based on outstanding achievements in maintenance (combat readiness), rocketry proficiency, and flight safety.

On 5 July 1958 the Air Defense Command's 497th Fighter-Interceptor Squadron arrived at Torrejón from Geiger AFB, Washington. It had an air defense role with North American F-86 Sabres. Many of the facilities were still under construction. The 497th FIS F-86Ds were transported to Spain by ship from Mobile, Alabama.

In time, all the F-86Ds arrived from the States. Construction was completed and gear put away.

On 26 April 1960, the 497th FIS transitioned to the F-102A Delta Dagger and operated under SAC control until its transfer to the USAFE 86th Air Division (Defense) at Ramstein Air Base West Germany on 1 July 1960. This transfer was made in order that all USAF fighter assets in Europe could be concentrated in one command. It's operated F-102s until 3 June 1964, when the squadron was reassigned to the 8th TFW at George AFB, California as an F-4C Tactical Fighter Squadron. Its F- 102A aircraft were transferred to other USAFE FIS squadrons.

Operations

Served as an operational training unit, providing both

F-102 from the 497TH Torrejón AB, 1962

F-102 Delta Dagger from the 497TH FIS, Torrejón AB

cadre personnel and dive-bombing training for other bombardment units, 1942-1943. Moved to Harding Field, LA in Oct 1943 and became a replacement training (later, fighter pilot training) unit until inactivation in 1944. As part of Air Defense Command's Western Air Defense Force, performed alert commitment for the Portland area, 1953-1955. Trained with F-86 from 1955-1958, then moved to Spain in Apr 1958. Operated jointly with the Spanish Air Defense Command, standing alert and performing air Defense training 1958-1963. During this period, was runner-up twice for the Hughes Trophy, 1961 and 1962, and won the trophy for outstanding performance as an air defense squadron for 1963. After moving back to the US in Jun 1964, equipped with F-4 aircraft and took part in tactical exercises, operational readiness inspections, and proficiency training. Combat in SEA, Dec 1964-Jan 1973. During this period, the 497th flew "Night Owl" interdiction missions and armed reconnaissance, led Navy pathfinder missions to numerous targets, and the first B-52s to targets in North Vietnam. Retained a combat capability until the same day, 16 Sep 1974 that the 8th Tactical Fighter Wing, its parent unit, moved to South Korea. In 1978, the squadron was once again assigned to the 8th Tactical Fighter Wing when it was activated at Taegu AB, South Korea, sharing the base with the Republic of Korea Air Force (ROKAF). Aircrews trained to remain proficient in close air support, interdiction, and air-to-air combat skills until 1989. Coordinated combat training and exercises in PACAF, 1991-present.

Convair TF-102A Delta Dagger 55-4034, from the 497TH FIS, Torrejón AB, 1964

F-102 from the 497TH FIS, Torrejón AB, 1960

Convair F-102A Delta Dagger "Dog"
65th Air Division USAFE
497th Fighter Interceptor Squadron (FIS)
Torrejón AB, España 1960-1964.

Chapter VII

United States Air Force in Europe (USAFE)

On 7 August 1945, United States Strategic Air Forces in Europe (USSTAF) was redesignated as United States Air Forces in Europe (USAFE). Its headquarters was relocated from Saint Germain-en-Laye, France, to Lindsey Air Station, Wiesbaden, Germany, on 28 September 1945. Within 18 months of VE-Day, virtually all U.S. armed forces personnel had left Europe except for the Occupation Forces in Germany, Austria, and a small number of Army troops in Trieste. USAFE had been reduced from a force of 17,000 aircraft and about 500,000 personnel to about 2,000 aircraft and 75,000 personnel. USAFE's four wartime Air Forces were demobilized or reassigned between August and December 1945. In March 1946 USAFE was given the status of a Major Command (MAJCOM).

A major postwar mission for USAFE was Operation Lusty, in which former Luftwaffe jet aircraft, such as the Messerschmitt Me 262A and Heinkel He 162A were located on various airfields around Munich and shipped to the United States for inspection and evaluation. At Lechfeld Air Base near Augsburg, large numbers of Me-262s were discovered, and valuable German air-to-air rockets. At the Oberpfaffenhofen air base near Munich - the former Dornier factory airfield, and today the home of Germany's DLR aerospace research facility - USAFE found a high-speed Dornier Do 335. This propeller-driven aircraft could reach a speed of 760 km/h, about 100 km slower than the Me-262 jet fighter. Other former Luftwaffe aircraft were collected and simply sent to blast furnaces for metal recycling.

In March 1947, General Joseph T. McNarney, Commanding General, U.S. Forces, European Theatre, told the War Department all he needed was "an Air Force of about 7,500 [men] to provide air transport and communications." He had no need for combat units, which he described as an "administrative burden," and he wanted them withdrawn. Nobody in Washington objected. Thus, the XII Tactical Air Command, the now USAFE combat organization after the inactivation of the four Air Forces, was inactivated on 10 May 1947. By this time, USAFE's fighting force appears to have dropped to a single unit, the 86th Fighter Group, which was shuffled around three separate stations in Germany in 1946–47 as it absorbed the inactivating personnel and equipment of first the 406th Fighter Group and then the 33rd Fighter Group.

In 1945 IX Air Force Service Command was reassigned from Ninth Air Force to USSTAF (about the date IX ASC moved to Erlangen). On 7 October 1946, IX ASC was redesignated European Air Materiel Command. This command administered USAFE's supply and maintenance depots. EAMC was headquartered at Erlangen Air Depot. At Erding Air Depot, it had Detachment B, 4th Air Vehicle Repair Squadron, and the 43d Air Depot. The 10th Air Depot was located at Oberpfaffenhofen Air Depot. The 862d Engineer Aviation Battalion and 837th Engineer Aviation Battalion were located at Landsberg. At Industriehafen Air

Depot was Detachment A, 42d Air Repair Squadron. Minor EAMC facilities were located at Bad Wiesse, Wolfgang, Munich, Bruck, Oberwiesenfeld and Bremerhaven. EAMC also controlled ammunition depots at Landesberg, Roth and Zepplenheim. EAMC remained assigned to USAFE until it was inactivated on 15 September 1947.

P-51D Mustangs, mostly from the 78th Fighter Group, in storage at RAF Duxford, England, summer 1945. Most of these aircraft were returned to the United States or used by USAFE units in Germany.

European Air Transport Service

The European Air Transport Service (EATS) controlled C-46, C-47 and C-54 transport aircraft and provided passenger and cargo transport within Western Europe. Its headquarters was at Wiesbaden. It initially controlled the former IX Troop Carrier Command squadrons which remained after the war. EATS operated both cargo and personnel transport routes in non-Communist controlled areas to support the American, British and French occupation forces, along with units in Greece (Athens Airport) and Italy.

Beginning of the Cold War

Concerned about the massive drawdown of USAFE and the United States Army Europe (USAREUR), the U.S. member of the Allied High Commission for Germany, John J. McCloy, had grave concerns that the troops available would be insufficient to ensure a peaceful transition in the American Zone. The United States' European wartime allies, Britain and France, had also rapidly demobilized.

In preparation for the future, the RAF and USAFE began a series of mapping flights over Soviet-controlled territory in Germany that led to numerous skirmishes and high tensions. Between the autumn of 1945 and 1947, mapped areas in west and central Europe, North Africa and the Atlantic Islands on a large scale in Operation Casey Jones. Casey Jones flights were made by reconnaissance variant RB-24 Liberators (the former "F-7" variant) and RB-17 Flying Fortresses (formerly called the "F-9"). These flights were only supposed to be flown over the Western Allies occupation zones, but there is a strong suspicion that these aircraft also operated over the Soviet zone. Soviet fighters regularly opened fire on American aircraft operating over their occupation zone. On 22 April 1946, a Douglas C-47 near the Tulln Air Base near Vienna over the Soviet zone of Austria was attacked by Soviet Bell P-39 Air cobra fighters. On 9 August, Yugoslavian fighters opened fire on another USAAF C-47 and forced it to land.

Rotation of strategic bombers through Europe

Soviet activity in Eastern Europe unsettled the western allies. President Harry S. Truman decided to take a hard line with Russia, lest the situation evolve into a new war. In Germany, Fürstenfeldbruck Air Base near Munich, Giebelstadt near Würzburg, and Rhein-Main near Frankfurt were rebuilt to accommodate Boeing B-29 Superfortress bombers. Strategic Air Command (SAC) wanted its B-29 fleet as close to the Soviet Union as possible because of their limited range and it was decided to rotate a portion of SAC's B-29 fleet through Europe. In November 1946, six B-29 bombers from SAC's 43rd Bombardment Group at Davis-Monthan Air Force Base, Arizona were deployed to RAF Burtonwood, England and from there to various bases in

Germany as a "training deployment." The B-29s were flown to bases in France, Turkey, Greece and were flown along the borders of Bulgaria and Russia over the Black Sea as part of "show the flag" operations. In May 1947, SAC began additional "training deployments" that stationed several B-29s in Germany at Giebelstadt and Fürstenfeldbruck. These B-29 squadrons were constantly rotated back to the United States being replaced with new squadrons in rotation. SAC also deployed B-29s to the United Kingdom where they were rotated through RAF Marham, RAF Waddington, RAF Scampton and RAF Lakenheath.

The United States also provided military aid to the Greek Air Force to help the nation resist the communists. AT-6 Texan trainers and C-47 Skytrain transport aircraft, along with armored vehicles, small arms weapons, munitions and radar were provided. In Turkey, various intelligence gathering aircraft were deployed along the northern Black Sea coast, providing the United States intelligence about the Soviet Republics of Armenia and Georgia. Overflights of the Soviet Union were also performed.

The Berlin Airlift

The Berlin Airlift was one of the defining events of and marked the beginning of the Cold War. The 464-day effort to supply a city's needs solely through the air demonstrated the resolve of democratic nations to oppose communist repression. The massive humanitarian effort was an early triumph for allied air forces and symbolized Western commitment to rebuilding democracy in Europe after World War II.

In 1945 the Soviets, Americans, British and French divided Germany into occupation zones. Berlin, although in the Soviet zone, also was divided among the four powers. On 18 June 1948, the three Western sectors agreed on a new common German currency, coming into force on 20 June that ended the use of occupation currency and introduced the Deutsche Mark. The Soviets considered this move a breach of agreements reached at the 1945 Potsdam Conference, which stated that Germany would be treated as one economic unit. In response to the currency reform action by the West, on 23 June the Soviets cut off electrical power to a large part of the western sectors of Berlin. The next day, 24 June the Soviet Union blocked western all road, rail and barge access through the Soviet occupation zone of Germany to the three Western-held sectors of Berlin, beginning the Berlin Blockade. The Soviets also now rejected western arguments of their occupation rights in Berlin, and legal claims to unimpeded use of the highways and railroads to the city.

USAF mobilization

After discussion of military options, the priority was given to supplying Berlin by air, as the Soviet blockade had little effect on the three Berlin air corridors. The Soviet Union did not initially interfere with the cargo aircraft flying the Berlin Airlift, as they were convinced that supplying two million Berliners by air was an impossible task. In 1948, USAFE strength was limited. The command consisted of 485 aircraft, with the 60th and 61st Troop Carrier Groups at Rhein-Main and Wiesbaden Air Bases near Frankfurt, both flying C-47s. The only other flying unit was the 86th Fighter Group at Neubiberg Air Base near Munich, with P-47s, which had been activated on 1 July 1948.

On the morning of 26 June, two days after the blockade began, the first C-47 loaded with milk and medicine took off from Wiesbaden Air Base for Tempelhof Air Base in Berlin. A total of 32 flights were made on that first day. Yet it would take many hundreds of cargo flights each day to provide the 12,000 tons of food, fuel, clothing and medicine it was estimated was necessary to sustain the two million people of western Berlin. There were simply not enough C-47s available, as it was estimated that over 900 would be needed to fly the necessary tonnage to Berlin each day. However, if the larger C-54 Skymaster was used, about 180 could supply the cargo necessary. However, there simply weren't that many aircraft available. The Military Air Transport Service (MATS) was ordered to mobilize all available C-54s and C-82 wherever they could in the world to support the airlift, and to refurbish as many as possible of the C-47s in storage at Davis-Monthan AFB for airlift duty. The C-74 Globemaster was also considered for use, as its massive cargo carrying capacity would drastically reduce the number of flights and aircraft necessary. However, the aircraft's landing requirements far exceeded what was available in Berlin, and it was unsafe to land it on the short runways. The C-74, however did fly cargo from the United States to staging bases in Europe.

To increase USAFE's tactical air strength, in July 1948 75 Lockheed F-80s were transferred to Germany with the 36th Fighter Group, being assigned to Fürstenfeldbruck Air Base, near Munich. This move considerably increased USAFE's tactical airpower, but also was considered as having great psychological value.

In August 1948, 10 C-54s arrived in Germany to begin airlift service. In addition, civilian DC-4s were loaned to the Air Force for airlift duty. The United States Navy provided 21 R-5Ds, their version of the C-54 as well. The airfields at Rhein-Main and Wiesbaden began to fill to capacity with planes, and the decision was made to also use Royal Air Force airfields at Celle and Faßberg. The U.S. Air Force, the U.S. Navy, and the British Royal Air Force together airlifted more than 2.3 million tons of food, fuel and medical supplies. Most of the tonnage was carried by the U.S. Air Force. The Berlin Airlift taxed existing USAF resources of cargo aircraft, aircraft engines, skilled aircrews, and maintenance personnel.

Strategic Air Command reassessed its B-29 forward deployments after the Berlin crisis arose. After initial forward deployments to Goose Bay Air Base in Newfoundland, and consideration of basing the bombers in Germany, it was decided to send them to Royal Air Force bases in Britain where they would be less vulnerable. The 28th and 307th Bombardment Groups were deployed to the newly activated station at RAF Marham.

Soviet Union reaction

After a few months it was clear to the Soviets that the Americans were succeeding in supplying the western sectors of Berlin with the minimal amount of supplies necessary to sustain it. Mock attacks by Soviet Air Force fighters begun in the air corridors to scare the American pilots caused great confusion and considerably increased the danger of air collisions. Also as many Yakovlev and Lavochkin fighters as possible were assembled around Berlin and then flown *en masse* in a westerly direction though the corridors. Near the western border of the Soviet occupation zone, they peeled off and flew along the zone border to the next corridor so they could fly back to Berlin along it, against the traffic, to their airfields around Berlin. Western radio frequencies were jammed, and chaff was released to confuse radar operators. Searchlights were shone on aircraft in the corridors at night. By the spring of 1949, USAFE announced that there were incidents of Soviets firing at cargo aircraft with anti-aircraft artillery, and of barrage balloons being allowed to float within the corridors. No serious aircraft accidents occurred as a result.

The efforts of many hundreds of pilots and the many thousands of military and German civilians involved in the airlift kept the people of Berlin supplied. On one day, the Berlin Airlift delivered nearly 13,000 tons of provisions with almost 1,400 flights. So great was the stream of aircraft that an aircraft landed almost once a minute at one of the three western Berlin airfields. The continuous engine noise of the aircraft stream of heavy transports not only made an impression on the citizens of Berlin, but on the Soviet Union.

The Soviet Union came to realize that the blockade of Berlin would not achieve the desired political effect they wished. On 12 May 1949, the Soviet blockade was lifted. However, airlift operated at a reduced level until the end of September to ensure adequate supplies were available in Berlin in case of a re-imposition of the blockade.

The 1950s

Even with the Korean War raging in the early 1950s, Europe received a higher priority of air power than Korea by the Truman Administration and the Department of Defense. In September 1950, the NATO Military Committee called for an ambitious buildup of conventional forces to meet the Soviets, subsequently reaffirming this position at the February 1952 meeting of the North Atlantic Council in Lisbon. This meeting established a goal of ultimately fielding 96 divisions in the event of a conventional war in 1954. As part of this buildup USAFE was intended to expand from 16 wings totaling 2,100 aircraft, to 28 wings, 22 of them in the Allied Forces Central Europe area alone, backed by deployed Strategic Air Command units sent from the United States.

The USAF transferred thirteen combat wings from Tactical Air Command plus one air depot wing from Air Material Command, and relocated the units to USAFE during the period from April 1951 through December 1954. Eight wings were regular Air Force wings, four wings were federalized Air National Guard units, and one wing was a mobilized Air Force Reserve unit. Four of these wings deployed to the United Kingdom, three into West Germany, and six wings were deployed to France. These wings numbered approximately 500 fighters, 100 light bombers, 100 tactical reconnaissance aircraft, 100 tactical airlift transports, and 18,000 personnel.

The 1960s. Berlin Crisis

The 1961 Berlin Crisis became USAFE's first test of what was known as a "Flexible Response" strategy. In the spring of 1961, Soviet Premier Nikita Khrushchev decided that the Soviet Union would sign a peace treaty with the East German government. In effect the German Democratic Republic would control the Russian zone of Berlin and could end joint occupation of the city. This action was a clear violation of the Potsdam Agreement of 1945.

When the Western allies objected to this proposed peace treaty, Khrushchev began speaking about restricting the West's aerial access to Berlin and preventing the entry of East Germans into the city. This possibility started an exodus of Germans from the eastern zone as they rushed to leave their sector and relocate in West Germany.

Departures snowballed from a few dozen refugees daily to a flow of 4,000 per day by August 1961. On the night of 12 August 1961 the Soviet backed East German government began erecting the Berlin Wall to prevent this flow of workers from communism, precipitating a new Cold War crisis that had been brewing for the previous twelve months. Berlin became a divided city. The response agreed to by the Kennedy Administration was to rapidly increase tactical airpower in Europe during the summer of 1961.

The Air Force responded with a two-phase deployment of reinforcements to Europe – the largest such overseas movement of aircraft since World War II. The first phase began on 5 September with Operation Tack Hammer. Tactical Air Command launched eight F-100D squadrons from its Composite Air Strike Force to augment USAFE strength with 144 fighters. All Tack Hammer fighters moved across the Atlantic Ocean with aerial refueling *en route*. The TACK HAMMER deployment was an interim measure until ANG units could relieve Tactical Air Command squadrons. The Air National Guard was tasked to supply six tactical fighter wings and one tactical reconnaissance wing to expand USAFE. Also deployed to Europe was the ANG 152d Tactical Control Group consisting of six Tactical Control Squadrons, manned by 230 officers and 1,850 airmen with mobile ground radar and radio equipment to control tactical air power on the battlefield. It was dispersed throughout West Germany.

The second phase began with the movement of eleven Air National Guard squadrons in late October and November 1961. Operation Stair Step was the code name for the rapid aerial movement of the fighters to Europe. Aircraft supplied by ANG wings totaled one hundred tour F-84Es, twenty RF-84Fs, seventy-eight F-86Hs, and seventy-two F-104As. Most of the fighters arrived on 4 November and amazingly had no losses *en route*. The F-84E and F-86Fs were considered old and obsolete aircraft even though they were only seven to nine years out of the factory. The three F-104 squadrons were activated on 1 November 1961. They disassembled their Starfighters and loaded them into Military Air Transport Service C-124s which delivered them to air bases in Germany and Spain.

French withdrawal from NATO's military structure

On 7 March 1966, French President Charles de Gaulle announced that France would withdraw from NATO's integrated military structure. He gave NATO forces one year (until 1 April 1967) to depart France. The United States Department of State, Department of Defense, and Air Force carefully managed the news about the American departure from France, and the attendant problems of an integrated NATO air defense for Western Europe and the decrease in tactical airpower. However, the news media were focusing on Vietnam, so the removal of NATO forces from France went virtually unreported in the US.

During 1966–67 all USAF offices and facilities in France were closed and personnel and equipment moved to other NATO countries. The last USAFE activities were the 1630th Air Base Squadron at Orly Airport and the Paris Administration Office. Both were closed in June 1967. A C-47 variant, the C-117B "Super Skytrain", was the last USAF aircraft to depart France on 31 May 1967. With the French departure, a major reorganization of USAFE was needed. The 49th TFW's three squadrons at Spangdahlem Air Base, and the 417th TFS of the 50th TFW at Hahn Air Base, were recalled to the US. Although the squadrons were relocated to the US, they were still part of USAFE's permanent force. According to the Department of Defense, these squadrons were 'dual-based'; they could return to their European bases at any given moment without lengthy preparations being necessary.

Although the withdrawal of USAFE forces from France was completed in 1967, it took until the mid-1970s until USAFE fully realigned its forces in Europe. Zweibrücken AB in West Germany and RAF Upper Heyford in England came under USAFE control within the next several years.

USAFE in Spain

Before Spain joined NATO in 1982, the USAF had for many years used Spanish air bases. Initially used primarily by the Strategic Air Command, they were Morón Air Base, at Morón near Sevilla in southern Spain, and Torrejón Air Base at Torrejón near Madrid. The Spanish air bases were important for reinforcing USAFE via the southern Atlantic route. Aircraft that flew to Europe via Lajes Field in the Azores always made a refueling stop at Morón, and later at Torrejón as well. These bases also had American facilities for carrying out aircraft maintenance and repairs. Yet it was primarily the good weather that drew USAFE to Spain for weapons training, which at that time was still mainly held in Libya utilizing the ranges at Wheelus Air Base.

As the American-Libyan relationship worsened throughout the second half of the 1960s, a growing number of USAFE fighter-bomber squadrons in England and Germany went to Zaragoza and gunnery ranges in Spain for weapons training. Zaragoza later became an important weapons training site for the USAFE and was also visited by F-15 Eagle squadrons for "Dissimilar Air Combat Training". During these air combat training exercises, the F-15s often practiced against Spanish Air Force Dassault Mirage F-1 fighters

In April 1966, the 16th Air Force was transferred from SAC to the USAFE, with USAFE taking control of the Spanish air bases at Zaragoza and Morón. Under USAFE, the Spanish bases became host to a growing number of deployments from CONUS. Morón received regular visits from Lockheed F-104C Starfighters of the 479th TFW from George AFB, California. During the Cuban Missile Crisis, a squadron of F-104Cs was stationed at Morón. Concern at the height of the crisis led to these aircraft being transferred to Hahn Air Base in West Germany, where they strengthened the air defense of central Europe. Sometime later, when the crisis had passed, the aircraft returned to the US via Morón. On 1 April 1963, their place was taken by F-105D "Thunderchief" fighter-bombers from the 4th TFW at Seymour Johnson AFB, North Carolina.

During the mid-1960s, the 16th Air Force also gradually took over responsibility for all USAFE operations around the Mediterranean.

USAFE in Turkey

The U.S. Logistics Group (TUSLOG) was the primary USAF agency in Turkey. TUSLOG not only commanded various USAFE units, but also supported all other U.S. military organizations and government agencies in Turkey. TUSLOG was established in 1955 and was headquartered in the Turkish capital of Ankara. The 39th Air Base Wing at Incirlik Air Base near Adana supported training deployments and regional exercises; communications for National Command Authority taskings; providing support for various units and an Air Mobility Command tenant unit providing air transport of passengers and cargo. From the 1950s – 1970s, the 39th supported various SAC activities in Turkey, which used Incirlik intensively as a base for U-2 reconnaissance flights along the Soviet border and in the Middle East.

In Ankara, the 7217th Air Base Group managed the logistical support for more than 40 units and agencies, as well as the needs of the American Embassy and U.S. Defense Attaché Office. From Izmir Air Station, the 7266th Air Base Group supported the two NATO headquarters, Allied Land Forces South-Eastern Europe (LANDSOUTHEAST) and the Sixth Allied Tactical Air Force (6 ATAF). The 7241st Air Base Group was the only U.S. military unit in Turkey not located at a single site but was scattered about İzmir in various locations.

In 1966, Senate majority leader Mike Mansfield began a campaign to unilaterally reduce U.S. troop levels in Europe. Following this, Secretary of Defense Clark Clifford initiated a program for the Reduction of Costs and Forces in Europe (REDCOSTE) in 1968. Although a change in administrations occurred in the same year, this program conformed to the Nixon Administration policy of lowering the profile of American forces abroad. Consequently, the U.S. began to eliminate or consolidate many of its operations in Turkey. Between 1969 and 1973, sites at Samsun and Trabzon were turned over to the Turkish government. In addition, Cigli Air Base, which since 1963 had been used by USAF rotational squadrons, was turned over to the Turkish Air Force in 1970. The U.S. continued, however, to fund the maintenance of numerous facilities there. Altogether, between 1967 and 1970, the number of Americans in Turkey dropped from 24,000 to 15,000.

The cutbacks in forces in Turkey naturally had a major effect on TUSLOG. The headquarters in Ankara shrank to a fraction of its former size. On 9 September, it was inactivated as the 7217th Air Division and the next day reestablished as Detachment 1 of Headquarters, Sixteen Air Force.

The 1970s and 1980s

Changes continued through the early 1970s. Headquarters USAFE transferred from Lindsey Air Station, Germany, to Ramstein Air Base in March 1973 and NATO's Allied Air Forces Central Europe was established at Ramstein Air Base in June 1974. The USAFE commander in chief then took command of Allied Air Forces Central Europe, in addition to commanding U.S. Air Force units in Europe.

In 1976, the new McDonnell Douglas F-15A Eagle air superiority fighter was introduced into USAFE service. The

Soviet Union's new MiG and Sukhoi fighters made the U.S. Department of Defense anxious. The Mikoyan-Gurevich MiG-25 'Foxbat' made them pull out all the stops to get the F-15A into USAFE. The F-15A was deployed to Germany in April 1977 with the 36th TFW at Bitburg Air Base West Germany. The 32nd TFS at Soesterberg AB Netherlands was also upgraded to the McDonnell-Douglas F-15A Eagle as part of Project Ready Eagle. By 1986, all USAFE F-4 wings were replaced by F-15 and F-16 fighters. The 36th TFW's existing F-4E Phantoms were incorporated into three new USAFE squadrons which were established at Hahn Air Base (313th TFS), Spangdahlem Air Base (480th TFS) and Ramstein Air Base (512th TFS). Preparations for the switch to the F-15 went ahead at full speed. Its introduction to the USAFE was given the project name `Ready Eagle' and, naturally, included transition training for the USAFE pilots.

This retraining was the joint responsibility of USAFE and TAC and first began in January 1976 at Langley AFB, Virginia, where the 1st TFW, was stationed. At Langley AFB, the USAFE's future F-15 pilots were given a crash course that familiarized them with the new aircraft in a relatively short time. The first F-15As arrived at Bitburg AB on 7 January 1977. These were two TF-15A (later redesignated as F-15B) trainers that had flown non-stop from Langley AFB in seven and a half hours.

These Eagles were to be used primarily for ground crew familiarization in anticipation of the arrival of the 525th TFS's first F-15As. The 23 aircraft for this first operational squadron left Langley AFB on 27 April 1977 for a mass Atlantic crossing. Over the following months, the aircraft for two other squadrons (22nd TFS and 53rd TFS) arrived. The 36th TFW's full strength of 79 fully operational F-15As was reached in December 1977. Project Ready Eagle was completed in precisely one year.

However, after flying the F15A and F-15B for just 18 months, the USAFE exchanged these models for the newer F-15C and F-15D Eagles. In May 1980, the 32nd flew five of its F-15A/B Eagles to Eglin AFB, Florida to participate in the weapons systems evaluation program. While at Eglin AFB, the united swapped its aircraft for the newer models. These planes arrived at Soesterberg AB on 13 June, making the 32d the first unit in the USAFE to be equipped with the latest versions of the F-15. The 32nd completed the upgrade on 25 November 1980. At that time the squadron possessed eighteen F-15C and two twin-seat F-15D fighter aircraft.

Post–Cold War era

USAFE never had to fight the Soviet Armed Forces and the Warsaw Pact states in Europe. The Soviet Union collapsed in 1990-91. The end of the Cold War saw a clamoring for a "peace dividend", and questions from many U.S. and Western European officials about the appropriate size and purpose of American military forces in Europe.

All American military forces, and those of the NATO organization as well, experienced rapid change. USAFE shrunk from over 850 aircraft and 72,000 personnel scattered among 27 bases in 1990 to approximately 240 aircraft, 33,000 personnel, and six flying bases by the end of 1996. In July 1994, with President Clinton in attendance, the British, French, and American air and land forces in

Berlin were inactivated in a ceremony on the Four Ring Parade field at Tempelhof Central Airport.

USAFE Headquarter. Ramstein Air Base gate

Chapter VIII

625TH Military Airlift Support Squadron (MASS)

The 625th MILITARY AIRLIFT SUPPORT SQUADRON (MASS) was activated on 8 January 1966 at Torrejón Air Base, Spain. It was an overseas unit of the Military Airlift Command (MAC) that was assigned to the 322nd Airlift Division (ALD) located at Ramstein Air Base, Germany.

On 24 December 1968, control over the 625th MASS was transferred from the 322nd ALD to the 435th Military Airlift Support Wing, which later was renamed the 435th Tactical Airlift Wing at Rhein-Main Air base, Germany. Ten years later, in 1978, the 625th MASS was reassigned back to the 322nd ALD. On 1 August 1983 the 625th MASS was deactivated, and two new squadrons were formed-the 625th Consolidated Aircraft Maintenance Squadron (CAMS) and the 625th Aerial Port Squadron (APS). These two new squadrons combined with the airlift coordination center and the forward supply location to form the new 625th Military Airlift Support Squadron Group (MASG), with the deactivation of the 322nd ALD on 1 April 1992, the 625th MASG began reporting directly to HQ 21st Air Force at McGuire AFB, NJ, effective 1 June 1992, with the activation of Air Mobility Command and the reorganization of the overseas in route support structure, the 625th MASG and its two squadrons, the 625th CAMS

C-5 Galaxy in Torrejón Air Base Flight line, 1986

C-5 Galaxy taking off from Torrejón AB, 1990

and the 625th APS were deactivated and in its place, the 625th Airlift Support Squadron (ALSS) was activated at Torrejón Air Base, Spain. At that time, the 625th ALSS began reporting to the 608th Airlift Support Group (ALSG) at Ramstein Air Base, Germany.

On 1 April 1994, the 625th ALSS was deactivated at Torrejón Air Base and the 625th Air Mobility Support Squadron (AMSS) was activated at Naval Air Station Rota, Spain.

The 608th ALSG changed their name to the 621st Air Mobility Support Group (AMSG)

Note: The 625th was a vital squadron for Operations Desert Shield / Desert Storm.

C-141 taking off from Torrejón Air Base early 1980's

C-130 Torrejón AB flight line, 1991

Chapter IX

401ST TACTICAL FIGHTER WING

The Group was first activated as the 401st Bombardment Group, March 1943 at Ephrata Army Air Base Washington. Its original squadrons were the 612th, 613th, 614th and 615th Bombardment Squadrons.

The initial cadre for the group was drawn from the 395th Bombardment Group at Ephrata and the 383d Bombardment Group at Rapid City Army Air Field, South Dakota. The cadre soon departed for Orlando Army Air Base, Florida, where they conducted simulated combat missions with the Army Air Forces School of Applied Tactics out of Brooksville Army Air Field.

The ground echelon moved to Geiger Field, Washington in May 1943 and to Great Falls AAB, Mount in July. At Great Falls the first combat crews were assigned to the group. In the final stage of training the squadrons dispersed with the 612th remaining at Great Falls, while the 613th trained at Cut Bank Army Air Field, the 614th at Glasgow Army Air Field, and the 615th at Lewiston Army Air Field

After completing training, the ground echelon left for overseas on 19 October 1943. After staging at Camp Shanks, New York they embarked on the RMS Queen Mary and sailed on 27 October disembarking at Greenock on the

Firth of Clyde on 3 November 1943. The air echelon staged for deployment at Scott Field, Illinois then flew to England under the control of Air Transport Command via Newfoundland, Iceland and Scotland.

Combat in the European Theater

On arrival in England, half of the group's aircrews were immediately reassigned to the 351st Bombardment Group. The rest of the group became part of Eighth Air Force at RAF Deenethorpe. The 401st was assigned to the 92d Combat Bombardment Wing of the 1st Bombardment Division. Its tail code was Triangle-S.

On 26 November the 401st flew its first combat mission against Bremen, Germany. It did not suffer the combat loss of an airplane until its ninth mission on 30 December. The 401st BG operated chiefly against strategic targets, bombing industries, submarine facilities, shipyards, missile sites, marshalling yards, and airfields. On 11 January 1944 the group led the 1st Bombardment Division in an attack against aircraft manufacturing facilities at Ochsersleben, Germany. Although the bombers were able to attack, poor weather conditions prevented the division from receiving effective fighter cover. For over three hours the bomber formation suffered more than 400 attacks by Luftwaffe fighters, including air-to-air rocket attacks. Despite these attacks the unit was continued its attack and struck a telling blow against German aircraft production for which the group was awarded the Distinguished Unit Citation (DUC).

A little over a month later, on 20 February, the group earned its second DUC for an attack on the Erla

Maschinenwerke aircraft manufacturing facilities in Leipzig, Germany. Despite fighter attacks and battle damage to the group's planes, 100% of the group’s bombs fell within 1000 feet of the aiming point. Beginning in October 1944, the unit concentrated its attacks on Axis oil reserves.

In addition to strategic missions, group operations included attacks on transportation, airfields, and fortifications prior to the Normandy invasion. On D-Day the 401st attacked Normandy beachhead areas dropping bombs five minutes before troops landed. The following month it provided close air support for the breakthrough at Saint-Lô, it also supported the siege of Brest in August and Operation Market Garden in September. During the Battle of the Bulge in December 1944 and January 1945, the unit attacked transportation and communications in the battle area. It supported airborne forces involved in Operation Varsity in March 1945.

The group's worst accident occurred in December 1943 when a Fortress which failed to get off the ground careened over farmland and came to rest after crashing into a cottage on the edge of the village of Deenethorpe. The surviving members of the crew just had time to evacuate the wreckage and warn the villagers of the imminent explosion of the bomb load before it detonated damaging many houses in the village. The blast was felt in Kettering nine miles away.

Lt Carl Hoag, a navigator with the group was awarded the Distinguished Service Cross for navigating his damaged plane back to UK from a mission to Bohlen. Lt Hoat was blinded in one eye and his vision in other eye impaired by injury. Despite these injuries, he was able to provide the pilot with directions to safely return the plane and crew to Deenthorpe.

The group flew its last combat mission on 20 April 1945 against Brandenberg. The group had flown 254 combat missions from Deenethorpe airfield, 91 aircraft were lost in action with the lowest loss rate of any group in Eighth Air Force. The group's heaviest combat loss had occurred on 28 May 1944 when it lost seven aircraft.

After V-E Day, the group flew missions to Linz, Austria to evacuate British and French prisoners of war. It also flew Trolley sightseeing missions at low level, flying ground support personnel over the Ruhr and Frankfurt am Main to see the damage that had been done as a result of their efforts.

The group was alerted for redeployment to the Pacific Theater and the last plane departed Deenethorpe on 3 June. The ground echelon sailed on the RMS Queen Elizabeth on the fifth. Upon arrival in the US, personnel were granted thirty days leave, reassembling at Sioux Falls Army Air Field, South Dakota, but plans had changed and personnel were either transferred to Boeing B-29 Superfortress units or processed for discharge and the group was inactivated.

Air Force Reserve

During the early years of the Cold War the unit was redesignated as the 401st Bombardment Group, Very Heavy and was allotted to the Air Force Reserve. It was activated on 26 June 1947 by Air Defense Command at Brooks Field, Texas, but there is no indication the group was fully manned or equipped. The 401st was redesignated the **401st Bombardment Group**, Medium in June 1949 and moved to Biggs AFB, Texas where it became an associate of the active duty 95th Bombardment Group. The 401st was called to active duty on 1 May 1951 during the Korean War. Its personnel were reassigned to other units and it was inactivated on 25 June 1951.

Tactical Air Command

The 401st was redesignated as a Tactical Air Command Fighter-Bomber group in 1953 and activated on 8 February 1954 at Alexandria Air Force Base, Louisiana. The group was equipped initially with F-86F Sabres returned from combat in Korea. The group was assigned three of its old squadrons, the 612th, 613th and 614th Fighter-Bomber Squadrons. The group was attached to the 366th Fighter-Bomber Wing at Alexandria (later England AFB), and its mission was to perform advanced fighter training on high performance jet aircraft. In 1955, the group converted to Republic F-84F Thunderstreaks, performing its training mission until 25 September 1957 when it was inactivated and its component squadrons were assigned directly to newly activated 401st Fighter-Bomber Wing. At the same time the wing transitioned into the North American F-100 "Super Sabre" aircraft and gained a fourth tactical squadron, the 615th Fighter-Bomber Squadron. Less than a

year after activation, the wing and its squadrons dropped the "**Fighter-Bomber**" designation for "**Tactical Fighter**". In 1959 the 401st wing became the host organization for England AFB when the 834th Air Division and 366th Tactical Fighter Wing inactivated.

F-84F-35-GK Thunder streak 51-9484

The 401st TFW Participated in numerous firepower demonstrations, tactical exercises and maneuvers in the United States and overseas, and periodically deployed its tactical squadrons to bases in Europe and the Middle East to support NATO. With the exception of its elements deployed overseas, the wing operated from Homestead AFB, Florida during the Cuban Missile Crisis from October to December 1962

From February 1964 to November 1965, wing's squadron deployments shifted to the Far East and Southeast Asia in support of operations in that area. In November, the wing's 612th Tactical Fighter Squadron moved to Misawa Air Base, Japan. The 90th Tactical Fighter Squadron was attached to the wing while it equipped with F-100s before moving to Bien Hoa Air Base, Republic of Viet Nam. The wing then briefly returned to support operations in Europe-Middle East. When the 614th and 615th Tactical Fighter Squadrons moved to Phu Cat Air

F-100D Super Sabre of the 401ST TFW

Base and Phan Rang Air Base in the spring of 1966, the wing was left with a single operational squadron. In 1966 fighter operations at England ceased and were replaced by special operations training. On 27 April the wing and its remaining squadron moved to Europe.

Torrejón Air Base

Prior to 1965, Torrejón AB hosted deployed squadrons of Boeing B-47 Stratojet aircraft rotating from CONUS Strategic Air Command (SAC) bases. Although B-47 deployments ceased, Boeing KC-135 Stratotanker deployments to support Operation Chrome Dome continued, but on a reduced basis, and the base was transferred to United States Air Forces Europe (USAFE). With the USAFE takeover of the base, the Air Force transferred the 401st Tactical Fighter Wing from England Air Force Base to USAFE on a permanent basis to Torrejón to perform host functions at the base and to support the rotational fighter deployments to Italy and Turkey for NATO alerts. The 613th moved with the wing, where it was joined by the 307th Tactical Fighter Squadron from Homestead AFB, Florida, and the 353d Tactical Fighter Squadron from Myrtle Beach Air Force Base, South Carolina. The wing's 401st Combat Support Group took over the support functions, personnel, and equipment of SAC's 3970th Strategic Wing

F-16 Fighting Falcon from the three Squadrons assigned to the 401ST TFW flying over the Sacedon lake in Spain.

In 1970 the 401st Tactical Fighter Wing (TFW) upgraded to the McDonnell Douglas F-4E Phantom II. In September 1973, an equipment changes to the F-4C model took place, then in 1978 to the F-4D.

As a result of the withdrawal of USAF forces in South Vietnam, in 1972 the 307th and 353d fighter squadrons were returned to their home bases, and the 612th and 614th Tactical Fighter Squadrons (TFS) were assigned to Torrejón. Also, in 1972, squadron tail codes were eliminated, and "TJ" became the tail code for all 401st TFW aircraft.

In 1983 the 401st upgraded to the Block 15 F-16A/B Fighting Falcon. The F-16s were upgraded to the Block 30 F-16C/D in July 1988.

In January 1988 Spain and the United States announced jointly that agreement had been reached in principle on a new base agreement with an initial term of eight years. The agreement essentially met conditions demanded by Spain that the USAF withdraw from a permanent presence on the base. The F-16 aircraft were to be removed from Torrejón by mid-1991. It was expected that this action would reduce the number of United States personnel in Spain by nearly one-half.

Implementation of this agreement was delayed by the 1990/91 crisis in Southwest Asia, when the 401st TFW was one of the first American fighter wings to respond. The 612th TFS deployed to Incirlik Air Base, Turkey as part of the 7440th Composite Wing (Provisional) and the 614th TFS deployed to Doha, Qatar where it became the core of the Tactical Fight Wing, 401st, Provisional, which was formed from the wing's support elements. However, after the 1991 cease-fire in Iraq, plans proceeded to close Torrejón Air Base.

Aviano Air Base

On 1 October 1991 the wing was redesignated the 401st Fighter Wing. Initially, the USAF decided to return the wing to the US and inactivate it. However, the remaining members of NATO lobbied to keep the 401st in the Southern Region OF NATO and offered to rebase it using NATO funds. In accordance with the 1988 agreement, the USAF portion of the base was returned to the Spanish government on 21 May 1992, and the 401st Fighter Wing transferred on paper to Aviano Air Base Italy without personnel or equipment. At Aviano it assumed the personnel mission and equipment of the 40th Support Wing, which was inactivated.

At Aviano, the 401st had no assigned tactical units, instead it supported rotating squadrons deployed there from other groups. The tenure of the 401st at Aviano AB was brief, as a result of Hurricane Andrew destroying Homestead AFB, Florida in August 1992. The 31st Fighter Wing, formerly at Homestead was transferred to Aviano on 1 April 1994, taking over the assets of the 401st Fighter Wing, which was inactivated.

Assignments

- II Bomber Command, 1 April 1943 - October 1943
- 92nd Combat Bombardment Wing, 1 November 1943
- 94th Combat Bombardment Wing, 8 January 1944 - 20 June 1945

- Army Service Forces (for inactivation), 1 August 1945 - 28 August 1945
- 44th Bombardment Wing (later 44th Air Division), 26 June 1947 - 25 June 1951
- Tenth Air Force, 27 June 1949
- Strategic Air Command, 1 May 1951 - 25 June 1951
- 9th Air Force, 8 February 1954 - 25 September 1957 (attached to 366th Fighter-Bomber Wing).
- 834th Air Division, 25 September 1957
- Twelfth Air Force, 1 April 1959 (attached to Air Division Provisional, 4481st, 1 January - 30 June 1964)
- 834th Air Division, 1 July 1964
- Sixteenth Air Force, 27 April 1966 - 1 April 1994

Aircraft

- Boeing B-17G Flying Fortress, 1942 - 1945
- North American F-86 Sabre, 1954 - 1955
- Republic F-84F Thunderstreak, 1955 - 1957; 1957
- North American F-100 Super Sabre, 1957 - 1970
- McDonnell Douglas F-4 Phantom II, 1970 - 1983
- General Dynamics F-16 Fighting Falcon, 1983 - 1992

Commanders

NAME	DATE
Colonel Neil B. Harding	circa 1 April 1943
Colonel Harold W. Bowman	June 1943
Colonel William T. Seawell	December 1944
Colonel Harry G. Libbey	26 June 1947
Lieutenant Colonel James L. Fletcher	circa October 1948
Unknown	27 June 1949
Lieutenant Colonel William N. Hensle	1 May 1951

Colonel Walter G. Benz	8 February 1954
Lieutenant Colonel Ralph F. Newman	1 March 1956
Colonel Chester L. Van Etten	2 June 1956
Brigadier General Ivan W. McElroy	1 April 1959
Colonel Albert W. Schinz	10 June 1960
Colonel Niven K. Cranfill	11 March 1962
Colonel Richard V. Travis	15 March 1962
Colonel William P. McBride	22 Sept 1964
Colonel Harold G. Shook	14 June 1965
Colonel Clayton N. Isaacson	7 May 1966
Brigadier General Sanford K. Moats	20 April 1967
Colonel Herndon F. Williams	2 November 1968
Colonel James N. Hoag, Jr.	8 January 1970
Colonel Wilbur L. Creech	17 November 1970
Colonel Tony H. Greget	19 July 1971
Colonel Richard G. Collins	6 September 1972
Colonel Charles L. Donnelly, Jr.	1 November 1973
Colonel Benjamin B. Battle	17 July 1975
Colonel Anthony T, Sheehan	14 July 1977
Colonel Kenneth W. North	12 June 1979
Colonel Wilfred L. Goodson	8 May 1981
Brigadier General Albert L. Logan	25 January 1982
Colonel John C. Fryer, Jr.	29 June 1984
Colonel Walter C. Hersman	4 October 1995
Colonel Lawrence P. Farrell, Jr.	17 August 1987
Colonel Patrick W. O'Brien	10 August 1988
Colonel Jerry L. Nelson	16 July 1991

Emblem

SIGNIFICANCE: The emblem is symbolic of the wing's primary mission. The light blue background represents the sky, our primary theater of operations. The four lances denote the weapons stacked ready for instant use as needed. A black and white checkerboard battlefield, crossing the lances in a horizontal position, indicates the wing is willing to go into battle anywhere in the sky. The colors of the squadrons, attached to the wing, form a banner which sweeps across the entire emblem, indicating support to the overall mission.

APPROVED: 9 September 1955

MOTTO: **CAELUM ARENA NOSTRA**

"The Sky is Our Arena"

Chapter X

307TH TACTICAL FIGHTER SQUADRON

Initially established under Third Air Force in early 1942 as a fighter squadron at Baer Field, Indiana, flying some antisubmarine patrols in the Gulf of Mexico.

World War II

Deployed to the European Theater of Operations in June 1942 without aircraft as its Curtiss P-40 Warhawks and Bell P-39 Air cobras were deemed unsuitable for use against German aircraft in long-range bomber escort duties. Was re-equipped with RAF Supermarine Spitfire Vs and its pilots and technicians spent a two-month period undergoing intensive training in flying and fighting with RAF pilots in the British aircraft from airfields in southeast England. The squadron flew its first combat mission on 18 August 1942, when it attacked enemy positions in occupied France.

Assigned to the new Twelfth Air Force and deployed to Gibraltar in November 1942 as part of the Operation Torch invasion forces, initially operating from former Vichy French airfields in Algeria. Advanced east across Algeria

Standing L-R: Daryl Olsen, George Wilson, Louis Batson, B. V. Johnson, Bob Schoen, Carl Granberry, Jim Harwood, Tim Albritton, Willie Wilson, gap, Frank Giaco, Jim Brinkman, Jim Learmonth, Dick Brehm, Doc Holliday, Larry Jakus, Don May, Charlie Gulley

Kneeling Center: L/C Dick Hansen, Commander

307TH TFS, 401ST TFW, Torrejón AB, 15 July 1967

307TH TFS, 401ST TFW, Torrejón AB, 15 July 1967

and Tunisia during the North African Campaign, supporting the Fifth United States Army which halted Field Marshal Rommel's advance on allied positions.

Spitfires from the squadron provided support for Allied Forces as the Invasion of Italy began with the capture of Sicily, and later the landings by Allied forces in Fascist Italy, moving north supporting the Fifth Army during the Italian Campaign. As Allied bomber forces operating from Italy began the strategic bombing of Axis petroleum and communications facilities in central Europe and the Balkans, the squadron was re-equipped with the North American P-51 Mustang to replace the shorter-ranged Spitfire. In August 1944, the P-51's were involved in the invasion of Southern France. In December 1944, the first destruction of a German jet fighter by a 308th P-51 occurred, eventually operating from the Po Valley in Northern Italy at the end of the European War in May 1945

By war's end, the squadron had earned two Distinguished Unit Citations and was involved in eight campaigns. The squadron was largely demobilized during the summer of 1945 in Europe, a skeleton force returned to Drew Field, Florida in August, inactivating largely as an administrative unit in November

Reactivated from elements of several inactivating organizations in Germany in August 1946, performed occupation duty and operating early-model Lockheed P-0A Shooting Star jets from former Luftwaffe jet-capable airfields at AAF Station Giebelstadt and AAF Station Kitzingen. Returned to the United States in June 1947 without personnel or equipment which remained in Germany.

307TH TFS, 401ST TFW, over Torrejón AB, 1960

F-100 from the 401ST TFW Torrejón Air Base late 1960's

Cold War

Assigned to Strategic Air Command at Langley Field, Virginia as a fighter-escort squadron, equipped with straight-winged Republic F-84E Thunderjets. Assigned to Turner AFB, Georgia with mission of long-range escort of B-29 Superfortress bombers, later B-50 and B-36 Peacemakers as newer aircraft came into operation by SAC. Inactivated 1958 with phaseout of B-36 and end of SAC escort fighter concept.

Reactivated in 1959 as Tactical Air Command North American F-100 Super Sabre fighter-bomber squadron at George Air Force Base, California. Trained in tactical air support of ground forces, deploying to NATO bases for operational exercises. Reassigned to Homestead Air Force Base, Florida after the Cuban Missile Crisis, late 1962 to provide air defense of South Florida. Was deployed for 3 months to Southeast Asia, in 1964 as part of advisory forces operating against North Vietnamese and National Liberation Front forces in South Vietnam.

Reassigned to NATO, becoming permanently based at Torrejón AB, Spain in 1966 when SAC turned Spanish bases over to USAFE. Initially equipped with F-100s, in 1970 received McDonnell F-4E Phantom IIs. Reassigned back to TAC at Homestead AFB in 1971, as part of re-establishment of 31st TFW upon its return from duty in Southeast Asia. Was deployed to Thailand, July 1972, engaging North Vietnamese forces in northern South Vietnam in response to the communist spring offensive. Returned to the United States in the late fall, 1972.

307TH TFS flying in formation, 1970

F-4 Phantom from the 307TH TFS at Torrejón air Base, 1970

For the next 20 years, performed routine training and tactical deployments from Homestead, upgraded to the General Dynamics F-16A Fighting Falcon in 1988. At the end of 1986 the squadron and wing changed tail codes from ZF to HS which better matched the squadrons location in Homestead. Upgraded to receive Shaw AFB block 25s in August 1990. With the Gulf War build up and the 363rd TFW at Shaw AFB deploying to Saudi Arabia meant no more block 25s were available. With some F-16A/B block 15s still in service for the 307th TFS, it continued to operate both types.

When Desert Storm ended it was decided to convert the 31st TFW to block 40 F-16s instead. Up to this point about ten block 25s had reached the 307th FS and had been pained in 'Emerald Knight' markings. They were all sent to other units. Neither of the 31st TFWs other sister squadrons flew the block 25. In March 1991 the 307th began conversion to the block 40 version of the F-16. On 1 October 1991 the word 'Tactical' was dropped and unit became the 307th Fighter Squadron. By early 1992 the conversion to block 40 F-16s with the general-purpose role was complete.

Moved to Moody Air Force Base, Georgia in late August 1992 when Hurricane Andrew threatened South Florida. It was to be a temporary move to Moody, but Homestead AFB was so heavily damaged it was never re-opened for any of the 31st FW squadrons and was eventually turned over to the Air Force Reserve Command's 482nd Fighter Wing and renamed Homestead Air Reserve Base. After the destruction of Homestead AFB, the 307th FS was reassigned permanently to the 347th Operations Group at Moody. At this point the 'HS' tail code began to be replaced with a 'MY' tail code, with some block 40 F-16s were delivered right from the factory to the 307th Fighter Squadron's new home base. It deployed to Saudi Arabia from, March–June 1995 in support of Operation Southern Watch

Inactivated in 1995 when Air Combat Command temporarily closed down ACC operations at the base, temporarily turning Moody over to Air Education and Training Command as a training base

Torrejón Air Base, Spain, 27 April 1966 - 14 July 1971.

Chapter XI

353RD TACTICAL FIGHTER SQUADRON

Activated on 15 November 1942 at Hamilton Field, California, initially equipped with Bell P-39 Air cobras and assigned to IV Fighter Command for training. Moved to several bases in California and Nevada then to Portland Army Air Base, Oregon in June 1943 and re-equipped with new North American P-51B Mustangs.

World War II

Transitioned to the Mustang throughout the summer of 1943 the deployed to the European Theater of Operations, being assigned to IX Fighter Command in England.

In late 1943, the strategic bombardment campaign over Occupied Europe and Nazi Germany being conducted by VIII Bomber Command was taking heavy losses in aircraft and flight crews as the VIII Fighter Command's Lockheed P-38 Lightnings and Republic P-47 Thunderbolts lacked the range to escort the heavy Boeing B-17 Flying Fortress and Consolidated B-24 Liberator bombers deep into Germany to attack industrial and military targets. The P-51 had the range to perform the escort duties and the unit's operational control was transferred to Eighth

Standing L-R: Jack Cousyn, Jim Parker, Dave Craig, Bobby Ockerhausen, George Kranz, George Dooley (CC), Morgan Pummill (Ops), Wendy Turner, Walt Storer, Roy Moore, Bill Washburn, Steve Holland

Kneeling L-R: Jack Sanders, Rudy Bow, Les Burden, Mark Taylor, Dick Stevens, Bill Endres, John Granskog

353RD TFS, 401ST TFW, Torrejón AB, late 1966

F-100s from the 353RD TFS, Torrejón Air Base

Air Force to perform escort missions. From its base at RAF Boxted, the unit flew long-range strategic escort missions with VIII Bomber Command groups, escorting the heavy bombers to targets such as Frankfurt, Leipzig, Augsburg, and Schweinfurt, engaging Luftwaffe day interceptors frequently, with the P-51s outperforming the German Messerschmitt Bf 109 and Focke-Wulf Fw-190 interceptors, causing heavy losses to the Luftwaffe. Remained under operational control of Eighth Air Force until April 1944, when enough numbers of P-51D Mustangs and arrived from the United States and were assigned to VIII Fighter Command units for escort duty.

Moved to Advanced Landing Grounds in France beginning at the end of June 1944, moving eastwards to combat airfields and liberated French airports supporting Allied Ground forces as the advanced across Northern France. Later, in 1944, the squadron became involved in dive-bombing and strafing missions, striking railroad yards, bridges, troop concentrations, and airfields. Participated in attacks on German forces in Belgium in the aftermath of the Battle of the Bulge, then moved eastward as part of the Western Allied invasion of Germany. The squadron flew its last mission of the war on 7 May 1945 from the captured Ansbach Airfield. Remained in Occupied Germany as part of the United States Air Forces in Europe XII Tactical Air Command occupying force after the German Capitulation, being stationed at AAF Station Herzogenaurach. Was inactivated on 31 March 1946.

Standing L-R: Ron Hutchison, John Leventis, Bill Hamm, Dale Sprotberry, Jack Cousyn, Jackson Saunders, Quinton Davis, John Granskog, Sqdn Sec'y, Roy Moore, Les Burden
Kneeling L-R: Keith Lukens, Bill Barrineau, Walt McMurtry, Bill Endres, Mark Taylor, George Dooley (CC), Karl Toth, Don Hubbard, Warren Nash

353RD TFS, 401ST TFW, Torrejón AB, May 1968

F-100 from the 353RD TFS, 401ST TFW, over Spain

Cold War

Reactivated by Tactical Air Command, United States Air Force on 19 November 1956, being assigned to the reactivated 354th Fighter-Day Group at the new Myrtle Beach Air Force Base, South Carolina. Equipped with North American F-100 Super Sabre fighters, the squadron participated in exercises, operations, tests, and firepower demonstrations conducted by the Tactical Air Command within the US and abroad. The unit frequently deployed to Aviano Air Base, Italy and Wheelus Air Base, Libya. Was deployed to Europe during the 1958 Lebanon crisis and was moved to McCoy Air Force Base, Florida in 1962 during the Cuban Missile Crisis. During the Dominican Civil War, the squadron deployed eighteen of its F-100s to Ramey Air Force Base, Puerto Rico to guard against Cuban intervention in the war.

United States Air Forces in Europe

In 1966 the 353rd Tactical Fighter Squadron was reassigned to the 401st Tactical Fighter Wing, Torrejón AB, Spain when Strategic Air Command ended B-47 Stratojet deployments to the base and it was reassigned to the United States Air Forces in Europe.

The host 401st TFW was itself reassigned to Torrejón from England AFB, Louisiana, with its operational fighter squadrons being deployed to Pacific Air Forces in South Vietnam for combat missions during the Vietnam War. The 353rd, along with the 307th TFS from Homestead and 613th from England to provide the 401st a full complement of aircraft.

F-4 E Phantom II 353RD TFS, Torrejón Air Base Spain, June 1970

F-4 E Phantom II 353RD TFS, Torrejón Air Base Spain, 1971

At Torrejón, the squadron continued to fly the F-100D "Super Sabre." Major operations consisted of maintaining combat readiness; rotating units to other bases in Europe or the Middle East and participating in various United States Air Force, North Atlantic Treaty Organization and Spanish Air Defense exercises. In 1970 the squadron had its aging F-100 fleet replaced, being re-equipped with F-4D Phantom II aircraft, its personnel being drawn from existing USAFE squadrons or new assignments from the United States. The 353rd's F-4's were tail-coded TK, and from Torrejón, the squadron made periodic partial deployments to Wheelus AB, Libya and Incirlik AB, Turkey, for weapons training. Beginning in June 1970, the 401st TFW was re-equipped with F-4E's.

In 1971, the 612th and 613th Tactical Fighter Squadrons were reassigned back to the 401st TFW from their deployment in South Vietnam as part of the drawdown of USAF forces in Southeast Asia. As a result, on 15 July, the 353 TFS was inactivated and reassigned without equipment or personnel to the 354 TFW at Myrtle Beach AFB.

Torrejón Air Base, Spain, 27 April 1966 - 15 July 1971.

North American F-100 "Super Sabre"
F-100D-20-NA 55-3586
401ST Tactical Fighter Wing
353RD Tactical Fighter Squadron
USAF Europe
Torrejón AB, Spain, 1969

Chapter XII

612TH TACTICAL FIGHTER SQUADRON

The 612th Tactical Fighter Squadron is an inactive United States Air Force unit.

The squadron was first activated during World War II as the 612th Bombardment Squadron. After training in the United States it moved to England, where it participated in the strategic bombing campaign against Germany. It earned two Distinguished Unit Citations for combat action. Following V-E Day, the squadron was inactivated in England. It was briefly active in the reserves from 1947, becoming a corollary unit in 1949. In the spring of 1951, it was mobilized for the Korean War and its personnel were used to fill out other units before the squadron was inactivated.

The squadron was redesignated the 612th Fighter-Bomber Squadron and activated in 1954 at Alexandria Air Force Base, Louisiana. In 1965 in moved to Japan, but most of the squadron was assigned to a detachment located in Vietnam. In 1971 it formally moved to Vietnam for a few months before it moved to Torrejón Air Base, Spain, where it continued fighter operations until inactivating in 1991.

World War II

The 612th Bombardment Squadron was activated March 1943 at Ephrata Army Air Base Washington as one of the original squadrons of the 401st Bombardment Group. The initial cadre for the squadron was drawn from the 395th Bombardment Group at Ephrata and the 383d Bombardment Group at Rapid City Army Air Field, South Dakota. The cadre soon departed for Orlando Army Air Base, Florida, where they conducted simulated combat missions with the Army Air Forces School of Applied Tactics out of Brooksville Army Air Field.

The ground echelon moved to Geiger Field, Washington in May 1943 and to Great Falls AAB, Mount in July. At Great Falls the first combat crews were assigned to the squadron. In the final stage of training the squadrons dispersed with the 612th remaining at Great Falls, while the other squadrons trained at bases in Montana and Wyoming.

After completing training, the ground echelon left for overseas on 19 October 1943. After staging at Camp Shanks, New York they embarked on the RMS Queen Mary and sailed on 27 October disembarking at Greenock on the Firth of Clyde on 3 November 1943. The air echelon staged for deployment at Scott Field, Illinois then flew to England under the control of Air Transport Command via Newfoundland, Iceland and Scotland.

On arrival in England, half of the 401st group's aircrews were immediately reassigned to the 351st Bombardment Group. The rest of the squadron became part of Eighth Air Force at RAF Deenethorpe. The

612th became part of the 92d Combat Bombardment Wing of the 1st Bombardment Division. Its tail code was Triangle-S.

On 26 November the 612th flew its first combat mission against Bremen, Germany. The 401st group did not suffer the combat loss of an airplane until its ninth mission on 30 December. The squadron operated chiefly against strategic targets, bombing industries, submarine facilities, shipyards, missile sites, marshalling yards, and airfields. On 11 January 1944 the squadron was in the lead group of the 1st Bombardment Division in an attack against aircraft manufacturing facilities at Ochsersleben, Germany. Although the bombers were able to attack, poor weather conditions prevented the division from receiving effective fighter cover. For over three hours the bomber formation suffered more than 400 attacks by Luftwaffe fighters, including air-to-air rocket attacks. Despite these attacks the unit continued its attack and struck a telling blow against German aircraft production for which the squadron was awarded the Distinguished Unit Citation (DUC).

A little over a month later, on 20 February, the squadron earned its second DUC for an attack on the Erla Maschinenwerke aircraft manufacturing facilities in Leipzig, Germany. Despite fighter attacks and battle damage to the 612th's planes, 100% of the unit's bombs fell within 1000 feet of the aiming point. Beginning in October 1944, the unit concentrated its attacks on Axis oil reserves.

In addition to strategic missions, squadron operations included attacks on transportation, airfields, and fortifications prior to the Normandy invasion. On D-Day the 612th attacked Normandy beachhead areas dropping bombs five minutes before troops landed. The following month it provided close air support for the breakthrough at Saint-Lô, it also supported the siege of Brest in August and Operation Market Garden in September. During the Battle of the Bulge in December 1944 and January 1945, the unit attacked transportation and communications in the battle area. It supported airborne forces involved in Operation Varsity in March 1945.

The squadron flew its last combat mission on 20 April 1945 against Brandenberg. It had flown 254 combat missions from Deenethorpe airfield. After V-E Day, the squadron flew missions to Linz, Austria to evacuate British and French prisoners of war. It also flew Trolley' sightseeing missions at low level, flying ground support personnel over the Ruhr and Frankfurt am Main to see the damage that had been done as a result of their efforts.

The unit was alerted for redeployment to the Pacific Theater and the last plane departed Deenethorpe in early June. The ground echelon sailed on the RMS Queen Elizabeth on the fifth. Upon arrival in the US, personnel were granted thirty days leave, reassembling at Sioux Falls Army Air Field, South Dakota, but plans had changed and personnel were either transferred to Boeing B-29 Superfortress units or processed for discharge and the squadron was inactivated.

Reserve Operations

The squadron was activated at Brooks Field (later Brooks Air Force Base), Texas in June 1947 as a unit of the reserves. It trained under the supervision of the 178th AAF Base Unit (later 2593d Air Force Reserve Training Center) of Air Defense Command (ADC). It is not clear whether or not the squadron was fully staffed or equipped. In 1948, Continental Air Command assumed responsibility for managing reserve and Air National Guard units from ADC. President Truman's reduced 1949 defense budget required reductions in the number of units in the Air Force. As a result, in June 1949 the 612th moved to Biggs Air Force Base in June 1949 and became a corollary unit of Strategic Air Command's 97th Bombardment Wing, which was stationed there. The May 1949 Air Force Reserve program had called for this new type of unit, which was a reserve unit integrated with an active duty unit. The plan was viewed as the best method to train reservists by mixing them with an existing regular unit to perform duties alongside the regular unit.

All reserve corollary units were mobilized for the Korean War. The 612th was called up on 1 May 1951. Its personnel were used as fillers for other organizations and it was inactivated on 25 June.

Fighter Operations

The squadron was redesignated the 612th Fighter-Bomber Squadron and activated at Alexandria Air Force Base, Louisiana in February 1954. Initially equipped with North American F-86 Sabres, then with Republic F-84F Thunderstreaks, by 1957 the squadron was flying North American F-100 Super Sabres as the 612th Tactical Fighter Squadron. The squadron participated in firepower demonstrations military exercises and maneuvers, it deployed aircraft and personnel to Europe and the Middle East to support NATO. During the Cuban Missile Crisis, the squadron operated from Homestead Air Force Base,

Florida. By 1965, however, deployments had begun to the Pacific and Southeast Asia.

The squadron moved to Misawa Air Base, Japan in November 1965, where it was assigned to the 39th Air Division. From Misawa, the squadron deployed aircraft and crews to Detachment 2 of the 39th Division, located at Kunsan Air Base, South Korea. In 1966, the squadron deployed to Phan Rang Air Base, South Viet Nam. On 10 October, Detachment 1 of the squadron was formed at Phan Rang, where it came under the operational control of the 35th Tactical Fighter Wing. Although the squadron continued to exist as a paper unit at Misawa, all its resources were assigned to the detachment, which engaged in combat operations in Vietnam. Between June 1967 and April 1969, the detachment operated from Phu Cat Air Base under the control of the 37th Tactical Fighter Wing, before returning to Phan Rang.

In January 1968, the 39th Air Division was inactivated and the 475th Tactical Fighter Wing moved to Misawa. The squadron was reassigned, but remained a paper unit until March 1971, when it moved without personnel and equipment and replaced Detachment 1 at Phan Rang. The American presence in Vietnam was being reduced, however, and the squadron's time at Phan Rang was limited. Combat operations ceased in late June, and on 15 July the squadron moved without personnel and equipment for the second time.

The squadron moved on paper to rejoin the 401st Wing at Torrejón Air Base, Spain in July 1971, replacing the 308th Tactical Fighter Squadron and assuming its personnel and McDonnell F-4 Phantom IIs. The squadron deployed to advanced locations in Europe and the Middle East, where it stood alert status. In 1983, the squadron converted to the General Dynamics F-16 Fighting Falcon. It deployed its forces to Incirlik Air Base, Turkey in 1990, where they formed the 612th Tactical Fighter Squadron (Provisional) under the 7440th Composite Wing (Provisional). After return to Torrejón the squadron was inactivated in the fall of 1991 as the United States removed its combat units permanently stationed in Spain.

Assignments

- 401st Bombardment Group, 1 April 1943 - 28 August 1945
- 401st Bombardment Group, 26 June 1947 - 25 June 1951
- 401st Fighter-Bomber Group, 8 February 1954
- 401st Fighter-Bomber Wing (later Tactical Fighter Wing), 25 September 1957
- 475th Tactical Fighter Wing, 3 November 1965
- 35th Fighter Wing, 15 March 1971
- 401st Tactical Fighter Wing, 15 July 1971 - 1 October 1991

Aircraft

- Boeing B-17 Flying Fortress, 1943 - 1945
- North American F-86 Sabre, 1954 - 1955
- Republic F-84 Thunderjet, 1954 - 1957
- North American F-100 Super Sabre, 1957 - 1971
- McDonnell Douglas F-4 Phantom II, 1971 - 1983
- General Dynamics F-16 Fighting Falcon, 1983 - 1991

Emblem

APPROVED: 9 September 1955

F-4 Phantom from the 612TH TFS, Torrejón AB 1974

F-4 Phantom from the 612TH TFS, Torrejón AB 1975

612TH TFS F-4 Phantom maintenance on Flight Line, Torrejón 1976

A pair of F-4 Phantoms from the 612TH TFS taking off

612TH Tactical Fighter Squadron F-4 Phantom

612TH TFS F-4 Phantom

612TH TFS F-4 Phantom on the runway. Torrejón, 1977

612TH TFS F-4 Phantom from Torrejón at RAF Lakenheath Air Base, 1972

612TH TFS F-4 Phantom II from Torrejon Air Base in RAF Alconbury, 1977

McDonnell Douglas F-4C Phantom II
612 Tactical Fighter Squadron
401 Tactical Fighter Wing
USAFE
Torrejón Air Base, Spain

F-16A from the 612TH TFS at Torrejón Air Base flight line, 1983

612TH TFS F-16's at Torrejón Air Base, 1988

612TH TFS F-16A getting ready for take off, 1988

612TH TFS F-16's ready for launch

Two F-16's from the 612TH TFS Flying over a castle in La Mancha, Spain 1989

TJ F16A over Segovia, Spain 1985

A left side view of a 612TH Tactical Fighter Squadron F-16A Fighting Falcon aircraft as it maneuvers toward a target over the Gulf of Iskenderumn

An underside view of a 612TH Tactical Fighter Squadron F-16A Fighting Falcon aircraft as it banks left prior to attacking the Koyna Range. The aircraft is carrying Mark-82 500-pound practice bombs on the wing

F-16A block 15 #81790 of 401ST TFW based at Torrejón AB seen on a training flight on March 27th, 1987

F-16A from the 612TH TFS based at Torrejón AB seen on a training flight on March 27th, 1987

Two 612TH TFS F-16 with an Spanish F-4 from the 12TH Wing

An F-16 from the 612TH with an Spanish F-4 Phantom from the 12TH Wing

Lockheed Martin F-16 "Fighting Falcon"
401ST Tactical Fighter Wing
612ND Tactical Fighter Squadron
USAF Europe
Torrejón AB, Spain

Chapter XIII

613TH TACTICAL FIGHTER SQUADRON

The 613th Tactical Fighter Squadron is an inactive United States Air Force unit.

The squadron was first activated during World War II as the 613th Bombardment Squadron. After training in the United States it moved to England, where it participated in the strategic bombing campaign against Germany. It earned two Distinguished Unit Citations for combat action. Following V-E Day, the squadron was inactivated in England. It was briefly active in the reserves from 1947 to 1949, but does not appear to have been fully manned or equipped.

The squadron was redesignated the 613th Fighter-Bomber Squadron and activated in 1954 at Alexandria Air Force Base, Louisiana. In 1966 it moved to Torrejón Air Base, Spain, where it continued fighter operations until inactivating in 1991.

World War II

The 613th Bombardment Squadron was activated March 1943 at Ephrata Army Air Base Washington as one of the original squadrons of the 401st Bombardment Group. The initial cadre for the squadron was drawn from the 395th Bombardment Group at Ephrata and the 383d Bombardment Group at Rapid City Army Air Field, South Dakota. The cadre soon departed for Orlando Army Air Base, Florida, where they conducted simulated combat missions with the Army Air Forces School of Applied Tactics from Brooksville Army Air Field.

The ground echelon moved to Geiger Field, Washington in May 1943 and to Great Falls Army Air Base, Montana in July. At Great Falls the first combat crews were assigned to the squadron. In the final stage of training the squadrons dispersed with the 613th training at Cut Bank Army Air Field.

After completing training, the ground echelon left for overseas on 19 October 1943. After staging at Camp Shanks, New York they embarked on the RMS Queen Mary and sailed on 27 October disembarking at Greenock on the Firth of Clyde on 3 November 1943. The air echelon staged for deployment at Scott Field, Illinois then flew to England under the control of Air Transport Command via Newfoundland, Iceland and Scotland.

On arrival in England, half of the 401st group's aircrews were immediately reassigned to the 351st Bombardment Group The rest of the squadron became part of Eighth Air Force at RAF Deenethorpe. The 613th became part of the 92d Combat Bombardment Wing of the 1st Bombardment Division. The group's tail code was Triangle-S.

On 26 November the 613th flew its first combat mission against Bremen, Germany. The 401st Group did not suffer the combat loss of an airplane until its ninth mission on 30 December. The squadron operated chiefly against strategic targets, bombing industries, submarine facilities, shipyards, missile sites, marshalling yards, and airfields. On 11 January 1944 the squadron was in the lead

613th Bombardment Squadron B-17S

group of the 1st Bombardment Division in an attack against aircraft manufacturing facilities at Ochsersleben, Germany. Although the bombers were able to attack, poor weather conditions prevented the division from receiving effective fighter cover. For over three hours the bomber formation suffered more than 400 attacks by Luftwaffe fighters, including air-to-air rocket attacks. Despite these attacks the unit continued its attack and struck a telling blow against German aircraft production for which the squadron was awarded a Distinguished Unit Citation (DUC).

A little over a month later, on 20 February, the squadron earned its second DUC for an attack on the Erla Maschinenwerke aircraft manufacturing facilities in Leipzig, Germany. Despite fighter attacks and battle damage to the 613th's planes, 100% of the unit's bombs fell within 1000 feet of the aiming point. Beginning in October 1944, the unit concentrated its attacks on Axis oil reserves.

In addition to strategic missions, squadron operations included attacks on transportation, airfields, and fortifications prior to Operation Overlord, the Normandy invasion. On D-Day the 613th attacked Normandy beachhead areas dropping bombs five minutes before troops landed. The following month it provided close air support for Operation Cobra, the breakthrough at Saint-Lô, it also supported the siege of Brest in August and Operation Market Garden in September. During the Battle of the Bulge in December 1944 and January 1945, the unit attacked transportation and communications in the battle area. It supported airborne forces involved in Operation Varsity, the airborne assault across the Rhine in March 1945.

The squadron flew its last combat mission on 20 April 1945 against Brandenberg. It had flown 254 combat missions from Deenethorpe airfield. After V-E Day, the squadron flew missions to Linz, Austria to evacuate British and French prisoners of war. It also flew "Trolley" sightseeing missions at low level, flying ground support personnel over the Ruhr and Frankfurt am Main to see the damage that had been done as a result of their efforts.

The unit was alerted for redeployment to the Pacific Theater and the last plane departed Deenethorpe in early June. The ground echelon sailed on the RMS Queen Elizabeth on the fifth. Upon arrival in the US, personnel were granted thirty days leave, reassembling at Sioux Falls Army Air Field, South Dakota, but plans had changed and personnel were either transferred to Boeing B-29

Superfortress units or processed for discharge and the squadron was inactivated.

Reserve operations

The squadron was activated at Brooks Field (later Brooks Air Force Base), Texas in January 1947 as a unit of the reserves. It trained under the supervision of the 178th AAF Base Unit (later 2593d Air Force Reserve Training Center) of Air Defense Command (ADC). It is not clear whether the squadron was fully staffed or equipped. In 1948, Continental Air Command assumed responsibility for managing reserve and Air National Guard units from ADC. President Truman's reduced 1949 defense budget required reductions in the number of units in the Air Force, [19] and the 613th was inactivated in June.

Fighter operations

The squadron was redesignated the 613th Fighter-Bomber Squadron and activated at Alexandria Air Force Base, Louisiana in February 1954. Initially equipped with North American F-86 Sabres, then with Republic F-84F Thunderstreaks, by 1957. The squadron was flying North American F-100 Super Sabres as the 613th Tactical Fighter Squadron. The squadron participated in firepower demonstrations military exercises and maneuvers, and deployed aircraft and personnel to Europe and the Middle East to support NATO. During the Cuban Missile Crisis, the squadron operated from Homestead Air Force Base, Florida. By 1965, however, deployments had begun to the Pacific and Southeast Asia.

In April 1966, the squadron moved to Torrejón Air Base, Spain. From Torrejón, the squadron supported NATO by deployments to bases where they maintained an alert status. The squadron continued this operation until it was inactivated in 1991, except for a period in 1970 when it converted to the McDonnell F-4 Phantom II.

Assignments

- 401st Bombardment Group, 1 April 1943 - 28 August 1945
- Tenth Air Force, 10 January 1947
- 401st Bombardment Group, 30 September 1947 - 27 June 1949
- 401st Fighter-Bomber Group, 8 February 1954
- 401st Fighter-Bomber Wing (later Tactical Fighter Wing), 25 September 1957 - 28 June 1991

Aircraft

- Boeing B-17 Flying Fortress, 1943 - 1945
- North American F-86 Sabre, 1954
- Republic F-84F Thunderstreak, 1955 - 1957
- North American F-100 Super Sabre, 1957 - 1971
- McDonnell F-4 Phantom II, 1971 - 1983
- General Dynamics F-16 Fighting Falcon, 1983 - 1991

Emblem

APPROVED: February 1955

Captain Win Reither F-100 Super Sabre pilot, 613TH TFS, 1969

F-4D 401ST TFW, Torrejón AB, Spain

F-4 Phantom from the 613TH TFS Torrejón Air Base, 1975

McDonnell F-4D Phantom II, 1981

Flight line, F-4 Phantom of the 613TH TFS Torrejón AB, 1974

F-4 Phantoms from the 613TH TFS approaching Aviano AB, Italy

McDonnell Douglas F-4D Phantom II
613 Tactical Fighter Squadron
401 Tactical Fighter Wing
USAF Europa
Torrejón AB, Madrid, España.

Crewchief Launching out an F-16 613TH TFS at Torrejón

F-16 from the 613TH TFS on the runway Torrejón AB, 1988

613TH TFS F-16's flying over Spain, 1988

Busy Flight line. Two F-16's from the 613TH TFS and a C-141 Starlifter, 1989

613TH TFS F-16 landing at Torrejón Air Base, with Torrejón city apartment buildings in the background, 1988

613TH TFS flying over lake Sacedon Raider Magazine

An air-to-air-right side view of three 613TH Tactical Fighter Squadron F-16A Fighting Falcon aircraft flying in echelon formation near Mt. Etna. The aircraft are deploying to Incirlik Air Base, Turkey

A 613TH Tactical Fighter Squadron F-16A Fighting Falcon aircraft refuels from a KC-135 Stratotanker aircraft while en route to Incirlik Air Base, Turkey, on deployment. Six other F-16s await refueling

Two F-16 from the 613th TFS approaching to Incirlik AB, 1987

Two F-16's from the 613TH TFS Torrejón Air Base Flightline, 1988

613TH TFS landing at Torrejón Air Base, 1988

613TH TFS Hot Pit Refueling at Torrejón AB

613TH F-16A's at RAF Fairford, UK on Jul 15, 1985

Lockheed Martin F-16 "Fighting Falcon"
401ST Tactical Fighter Wing
613TH Tactical Fighter Squadron
USAF Europe
Torrejón AB, Spain

Chapter XIV

614TH TACTICAL FIGHTER SQUADRON

The 614th Tactical Fighter Squadron is an inactive United States Air Force unit.

The squadron was first activated during World War II as the 614th Bombardment Squadron. After training in the

United States it moved to England, where it participated in the strategic bombing campaign against Germany. It earned two Distinguished Unit Citations for combat action. Following V-E Day, the squadron was inactivated in England. It was briefly active in the reserves from 1947 to 1949, but does not appear to have been fully manned or equipped.

The squadron was redesignated the 614th Fighter-Bomber Squadron and activated in 1954 at Alexandria Air Force Base, Louisiana. After temporary deployments to Southeast Asia, the squadron moved to Phan Rang Air Base, South Vietnam. It engaged in combat operations until being withdrawn from the theater and moving to Torrejón Air Base, Spain, where it continued fighter operations until inactivating in 1992, as the Air Force withdrew permanently stationed units from Spain. Shortly before inactivating, its planes and pilots were used to man a provisional organization during Operation Desert Storm.

World War II

The 614th Bombardment Squadron was activated March 1943 at Ephrata Army Air Base Washington as one of the original squadrons of the 401st Bombardment Group. The initial cadre for the squadron was drawn from the 395th Bombardment Group at Ephrata and the 383rd Bombardment Group at Rapid City Army Air Field, South Dakota. The cadre soon departed for Orlando Army Air Base, Florida, where they conducted simulated combat missions with the Army Air Forces School of Applied Tactics out of Brooksville Army Air Field.

The ground echelon moved to Geiger Field, Washington, in May 1943 and to Great Falls Army Air Base, Montana in July. At Great Falls the first combat crews were assigned to the squadron. In the final stage of training the squadrons dispersed with the 614th training at Glasgow Army Air Field.

After completing training, the ground echelon left for overseas on 19 October 1943. After staging at Camp Shanks, New York, they embarked on the RMS Queen Mary and sailed on 27 October disembarking at Greenock on the Firth of Clyde on 3 November 1943. The air echelon staged for deployment at Scott Field, Illinois, then flew to England under the control of Air Transport Command via Newfoundland, Iceland and Scotland.

On arrival in England, half of the 401st group's aircrews were immediately reassigned to the 351st Bombardment Group. The rest of the squadron became part of Eighth Air Force at RAF Deenethorpe. The 614th became part of the 92d Combat Bombardment Wing of the 1st Bombardment Division. Its tail code was Triangle-S.

On 26 November the 614th flew its first combat mission against Bremen, Germany. The 401st group did not suffer the combat loss of an airplane until its ninth mission on 30 December The squadron operated chiefly against strategic targets, bombing industries, submarine facilities, shipyards, missile sites, marshalling yards, and airfields. On 11 January 1944 the squadron was in the lead group of the 1st Bombardment Division in an attack against aircraft manufacturing facilities at Ochsersleben, Germany. Although the bombers were able to attack, poor weather conditions prevented the division from receiving effective fighter cover. For over three hours the bomber formation suffered more than 400 attacks by Luftwaffe fighters, including air-to-air rocket attacks. Despite these attacks the unit continued its attack and struck a telling blow against German aircraft production for which the squadron was awarded a Distinguished Unit Citation (DUC).

614th Bombardment Squadron B-17G

A little over a month later, on 20 February, the squadron earned its second DUC for an attack on the Erla Maschinenwerke aircraft manufacturing facilities in Leipzig, Germany. Despite fighter attacks and battle damage to the 614th's planes, 100% of the unit's bombs fell within 1000 feet of the aiming point. Beginning in October 1944, the unit concentrated its attacks on Axis oil reserves.

In addition to strategic missions, squadron operations included attacks on transportation, airfields, and fortifications to support Operation Overlord, the Normandy invasion. On D-Day the 614th attacked Normandy beachhead areas dropping bombs five minutes before troops landed. The following month it provided close air support for Operation Cobra, the breakthrough at Saint-Lô, it also supported the siege of Brest in August and Operation Market Garden in September. During the Battle of the Bulge in December 1944 and January 1945, the unit attacked transportation and communications in the battle area. It supported airborne forces involved in Operation Varsity, the airborne assault across the Rhine in March 1945.

The squadron flew its last combat mission on 20 April 1945 against Brandenberg. It had flown 254 combat missions from Deenethorpe airfield. After V-E Day, the squadron flew missions to Linz, Austria to evacuate British and French prisoners of war. It also flew Trolley sightseeing missions at low level, flying ground support personnel over the Ruhr and Frankfurt am Main to see the damage that had been done as a result of their efforts.

The unit was alerted for redeployment to the Pacific Theater and the last plane departed Deenethorpe in early June. The ground echelon sailed on the RMS Queen Elizabeth on the fifth. Upon arrival in the US, personnel were granted thirty days leave, reassembling at Sioux Falls Army Air Field, South Dakota, but plans had changed and personnel were either transferred to Boeing B-29

Superfortress units or processed for discharge and the squadron was inactivated.

Reserve Operations

The squadron was activated at Brooks Field (later Brooks Air Force Base), Texas in January 1947 as a unit of the reserves. It trained under the supervision of the 178th AAF Base Unit (later 2593d Air Force Reserve Training Center) of Air Defense Command (ADC). It is not clear whether the squadron was fully staffed or equipped. In 1948, Continental Air Command assumed responsibility for managing reserve and Air National Guard units from ADC. President Truman's reduced 1949 defense budget required reductions in the number of units in the Air Force, and the 614th was inactivated in June.

Fighter operations

The squadron was redesignated the 614th Fighter-Bomber Squadron and activated at Alexandria Air Force Base, Louisiana in February 1954. Initially equipped with North American F-86 Sabres, then with Republic F-84F Thunderstreaks, by 1957. The squadron was flying North American F-100 Super Sabres as the 614th Tactical Fighter Squadron. The squadron participated in firepower demonstrations military exercises and maneuvers, it also deployed aircraft and personnel to Europe and the Middle East to support NATO. During the Cuban Missile Crisis, the squadron operated from Homestead Air Force Base, Florida. By 1965, however, deployments had begun to the Pacific and Southeast Asia.

In the spring of 1966, the squadron's parent wing (military aviation unit) moved to Torrejón Air Base, Spain, but the squadron remained at England Air Force Base until September, when it moved to Phan Rang Air Base, Republic of Vietnam and was assigned to the 366th Tactical Fighter Wing. Shortly after the squadron's arrival at Phan Rang, the 366th Wing moved on paper to Da Nang Air Base, and the 35th Tactical Fighter Wing became the squadron's new headquarters. The squadron continued combat operations in Vietnam until the 35th Wing stood down from combat on 26 June 1971.

The squadron moved on paper to rejoin the 401st Wing at Torrejón in July 1971, replacing the 353d Tactical Fighter Squadron and assuming its personnel and McDonnell F-4 Phantom IIs. The squadron deployed to advanced locations in Europe and the Middle East, where it stood alert status. It deployed its forces to Doha International Airport, Qatar in 1990, where they formed the 614th Tactical Fighter Squadron (Provisional). It flew 1303 sorties into Iraq and Kuwait, delivering 3.7 million pounds of weapons. It was the first USAF unit to ever deploy to Qatar. It was inactivated in 1992 as the United States removed its combat units permanently stationed in Spain.

Assignments

- 401st Bombardment Group, 1 April 1943 - 28 August 1945
- Tenth Air Force, 10 January 1947
- 401st Bombardment Group, 30 September 1947 - 27 June 1949
- 401st Fighter-Bomber Group, 8 February 1954

- 401st Fighter-Bomber Wing (later 401st Tactical Fighter Wing), 25 September 1957
- 834th Air Division, 27 April 1966
- 366th Tactical Fighter Wing, 18 September 1966
- 35th Tactical Fighter Wing, 10 October 1966
- 401st Tactical Fighter Wing, 15 July 1971 - 1 January 1992

Aircraft

- Boeing B-17 Flying Fortress, 1943 - 1945
- North American F-86 Sabre, 1954 - 1955
- Republic F-84F Thunderstreak, 1954 - 1957
- North American F-100 Super Sabre, 1957 - 1971
- McDonnell F-4 Phantom II, 1971 - 1983
- General Dynamics F-16 Fighting Falcon, 1983 - 1992

Emblem

APPROVED: October 1955

614TH TFS Lucky Devils

F-4 Phantom from the 614TH TFS over Torrejón Air Base, 1975

F-4 Phantom from the 614TH TFS being towed off the flight line, 1973

F-4 Phantom from the 614th TFS. Torrejón Air Base, 1975

An F-4 Phantom from the 614TH TFS flying over Italy

An F-4 Phantom from the 614TH TFS on final approach to Aviano AB, Italy

McDonnell Douglas F-4D Phantom II
614 Tactical Fighter Squadron
401 Tactical Fighter Wing
USAF Europe
Torrejón AB, Madrid, España.

An air-to-air right side view of two F-16A Fighting Falcon aircraft assigned to the 614TH TFS banking left during a training mission in 1985

An air-to-air left side view of two F-16A Fighting Falcon aircraft assigned to the 614TH TFS in formation during a training mission in 1985.

An air-to-air right side view of two F-16A Fighting Falcon aircraft assigned to the 614TH TFS executing a gradual climb during a training mission in 1988.

An F-16 from the 614TH TFS landing in Torrejón Air Base, 1986

F-16's from the 614TH TFS final approach to Torrejón

F-16 of the 614TH TFS prepared to land. Torrejón Air Base, 1988

Two F-16's from the 614TH TFS approaching Torrejón, 1988

One 614TH TFS F-16 and an F-16 from the 401ST Squadron Commnader just landed in Torrejón, 1988

Lockheed Martin F-16 "Fighting Falcon"
401ST Tactical Fighter Wing
614TH Tactical Fighter Squadron
USAF Europe
Torrejón AB, Spain

Chapter XV

401st Tactical Fighter Wing Contributions to Desert Shield/Storm

The 401st TFW deployed two Tactical Fighter Squadrons, the 612th TFS to Incirlik Turkey, and the 614th TFS to Doha, Qatar. Both flew daily missions into Iraq and Kuwait. The 614th TFS flew 1,303 combat sorties and dropped over 3.7 million pounds of bombs. The 612th TFS flew 1,093 combat sorties and dropped over 3.9 million pounds of bombs.

Torrejón Air Base and the 401st TFW support personnel at Torrejón Air Base supported 39 percent of the total airflow for Desert Shield/Desert Storm and Proven Force. By the end of April 1991, the 401st TFW had supported 10,235 missions through Torrejón Air Base and 92.000 passengers. This averaged 1,400 aircraft per month from August-February.

The 401st TFW Hospital deployed an Air Transportable Hospital to Qatar and were prepared to act as USAFE's only Southern Region aeromedical staging facility. A 250 bed ASF was readied and staffed with medical augmented from USAFE and the CONUS. The hospital personnel issued chemical warfare antidote kits to transiting personnel, operated a flight line sick call service, blood donor transshipment center, blood donor center, and was ready with a mobile decontamination team.

401st Supply Squadron supported Desert Shield/Storm by supplying fuel, supplies and spare parts to aircraft transiting Torrejón AB. The fuel supplied during Desert Shield/Storm peaked at 38 million gallons in January and by the cease fire had reached 185.5 million gallons since the beginning of Desert Storm. Supply provided 9,000 items and 3 million pounds of munitions.

The 401st Services Squadron provided 500,000 meals to transiting personnel and billeted over 345,000 aircrew members.

401st Civil Engineers built a field kitchen, and tumed a maintenance hangar into a troop reception center and a warehouse into an aeromedical staging facility.

A KC-135R Stratotanker refuels an F-16C Fighting Falcon fighter aircraft from the 614TH Tactical Fighter Squadron (TFS), 401ST Tactical Fighter Wing of Torrejón Air Base, Spain, as the other Fighting Falcon from the 614TH TFS fly alongside during Operation Desert Shield.

An air-to-air view of an F-16C Fighting Falcon fighter aircraft of the 614TH Tactical Fighter Squadron, 401ST Tactical Fighter Wing of Torrejón Air Base, Spain, during Operation **Desert Shield**.

An air-to-air view of a multinational group of fighter jets, including, left to right, a Qatari F-1 Mirage, a French F-1C Mirage, a U.S. Air Force F-16C Fighting Falcon from the 614TH Tactical Fighter Squadron, a Canadian CF/A-18A Hornet and a Qatari Alpha Jet, during **Operation Desert Shield**

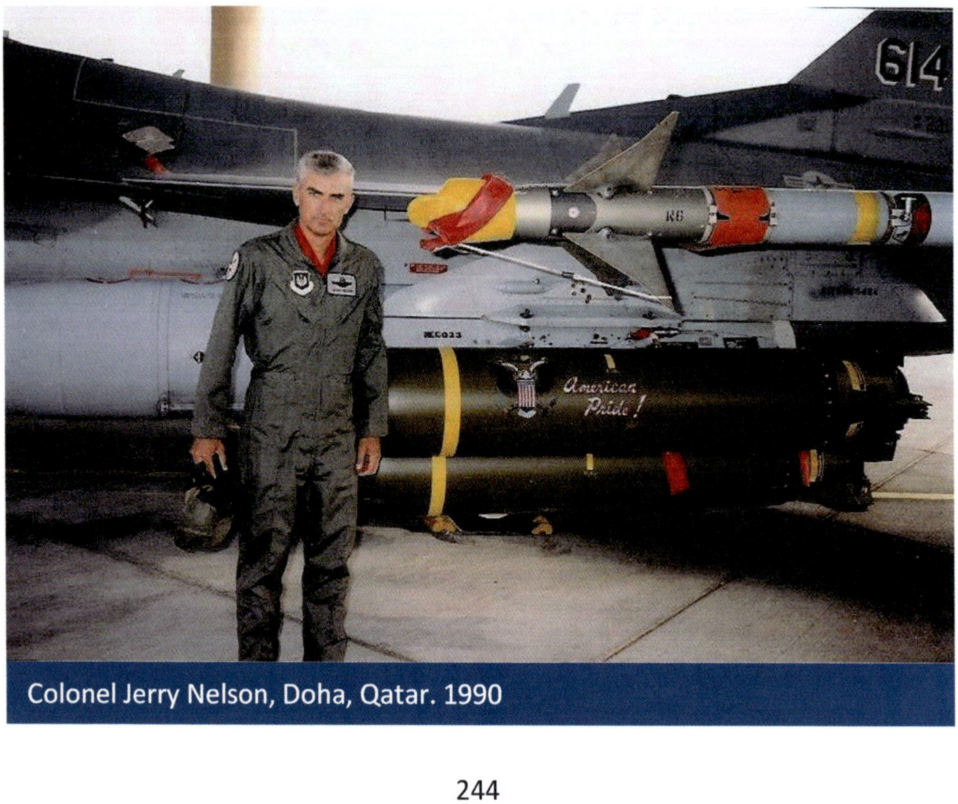

Colonel Jerry Nelson, Doha, Qatar. 1990

SSGT Alex de Jesus standing about 5 or 6 from right

TSgt Randy Couch, SSgt Alex De Jesus, SSgt Timothy Footman & SSgt Mike Gonzales

SSGT Alex De Jesus. Operation Desert Shield

Torrejón Air Base Desert Shield, 1990

Torrejón busy flight line during Operation Desert Shield, 1991

Torrejón Air Base during Operation Desert Shield, 1990

Torrejón Air Base Summer, 1990

Torrejón Air Base Flight line during **Desert Shield/Desert Storm,** 1990

Torrejón Air Base, Tarmac Desert Shield, 1991

An F-16C Fighting Falcon from the 614TH TFS, 401ST Tactical Fighter Wing taxis to the end of a runway during **Operation Desert Storm**

Munitions loading crews put a MK-20 Rockeye anti-armor bomb on the wing of an F-16 Falcon from 401ST Tactical Fighter Wing, Torrejón Air Base, Spain, at a base in Southeast Asia during **Operation Desert Storm**

SGT Emma Piehl center of the picture. **Operation Desert Storm**

Chapter XVI

Departure of the 16TH Air Force and 401st Fighter Wing

The 1988 Agreement

Following the death of General Franco in 1975, the United States welcomed the liberalization of the Spanish regime under King Juan Carlos and sought to bring Spain further into Western military arrangements. In 1976 the bilateral agreement between Spain and the United States was transformed into a Treaty of Friendship and Cooperation. In addition to renewing United States basing rights in return for United States military and economic aid, this treaty provided for a United States-Spanish Council intended to serve as a bridge to eventual Spanish membership in NATO.

During the early years of democratic rule, the government's focus was on consolidating the parliamentary system, and foreign policy issues received less attention. However, a point of contention persisted between the governing UCD and the Socialist opposition over Spain's relations with NATO and with the United States.

When Calvo Sotelo replaced Suárez as president in 1981, he made vigorous efforts to gain approval for Spanish membership in NATO, and shortly after this was accomplished a new executive agreement on the use of bases in Spain was signed with the United States in July

1982. This agreement was one of a series of renewals of the basic 1953 arrangement, providing for United States use of strategic naval and air bases on Spanish soil in exchange for United States military and economic assistance.

Many Spaniards resented the presence of these bases in Spain, recalling the widely publicized photograph of United States president Dwight D. Eisenhower, throwing his arms around Franco when the first agreement on bases was signed. There were occasional popular protests these reminders of United States support for the dictatorship, including a demonstration during United States president Ronald Reagan's 1985 visit to Spain.

The Socialists had consistently advocated a more neutralist, independent stance for Spain, and when they came to power in October 1982, President González pledged a close examination of the defense and cooperation agreements with the United States. A reduction in the United States military presence in Spain was one of the stipulations contained in the referendum, held in 1986, on continued NATO membership. In keeping with this, the President announced in December 1987 that the United States would have to remove its seventy-two F-16 fighter-bombers from Torrejón Air Base by mid-1991. Spain also had informed the United States in November that the bilateral defense agreement, which opinion polls indicated was rejected overwhelmingly by the Spanish population, would not be renewed. Nevertheless, in January 1988 Spain and the United States did reach agreement in principle on a new base agreement to last eight years. The new military arrangements called for a marked reduction of the United States presence in Spain and terminated the

United States military and economic aid that had been tied to the defense treaty.

USAF Withdrawal

The United States felt that even though Italy subsequently agreed to station the F-16 wing at Aviano Air Base, the cost of transfer would be high, and the unit would be in a more exposed position to Warsaw Pact forces.

In January 1988, Spain and the United States announced jointly that agreement had been reached in principle on a new base agreement with an initial term of eight years, essentially meeting the conditions demanded by Spain. The F-16s were to be removed from Torrejón within three years, by mid-1991. It was expected that this step would reduce the number of United States personnel in Spain by nearly one-half.

Implementation of this agreement was delayed by the 1990-91 crisis in Kuwait, when the 401st TFW was one of the first American fighter wings to respond, with the 612th TFS deploying to its wartime base at Incirlik Turkey and the 614th TFS becoming the first US Military unit to deploy to the Persian Gulf State of Qatar. Both squadrons flew a large number of operational missions during Operations Desert Shield and Storm.

After the 1991 cease-fire in Iraq, plans proceeded to close Torrejón Air Base. On 28 June, the 613th TFS was inactivated and its aircraft sent to Air National Guard squadrons in the United States. The 612th TFS inactivated on 1 October and the 614th TFS on 1 January 1992.

In accordance with the 1988 agreement, the USAF portion of the base was turned-over to the Spanish government on 21 May 1992, with the 401st Fighter Wing being transferred to Aviano Air Base, Italy without personnel or equipment.

Raider

March 27, 1992
Vol. 16, No. 19
Torrejon AB, Spain

Inside

Finance

Torrejon AB members' pay changes with cost-of-living allowances. **See Page 6.**

U.S. Air Force photo by TSgt. Ron Rush

Col. Jerry L. Nelson, 401st Fighter Wing commander, addresses Spanish news media regarding the final four F-16s leaving Torrejon AB. The departure of the aircraft ends the wing's 26-year flying mission at Torrejon.

Last four F-16s depart Torrejon

Colonel Nelson final speech to the Spanish Media before leaving to Ramstein, March 1992

Last four F-16s from Torrejón AB getting ready to leave after 26 years of proud service 1966-1992

Last four pilots from the 401ST FW at Torrejón AB, March 1992

Engine Start Last Flight. Colonel Wade Paton, 1992

F-16s last flight from Torrejón AB to Ramstein, March 1992

12TH Wing pilots getting ready to escort the 401ST FW F-16s. Colonel Francisco José Gómez Carretero 12TH Wing Commander, the first one from the right, March 1992

One of the four spanish F-18s from the 12TH Wing who escorted the F-16s of the 401ST FW to the French border as a symbol of friendship

One of the four spanish F-18s from the 12TH Wing who escorted the F-16s of the 401ST FW to the French border as a symbol of friendship

F-16 last flight from Torrejón AB to Ramstein, March 1992

Last flight, 24 March 1992

C-141 STARLIFTER Torrejón Air Base, March 1992

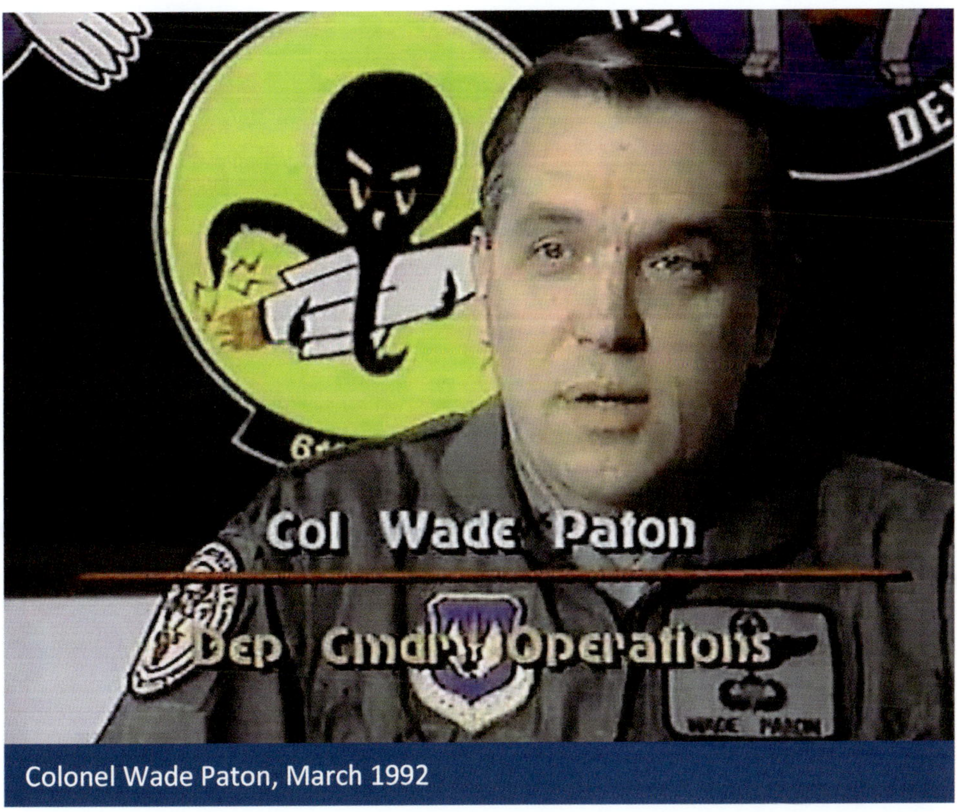

Colonel Wade Paton, March 1992

Chapter XVII

MISCELLANEOUS

Photographs

American actress **Ann Margaret** and a B-47 crewmember from the 351ST Bomb Squadron when she visited Torrejon in 1964. Major **Ed Michigan** was later killed, in Feb 1965, along with three other B-47 crewmembers, when the B-47 he was in collided with a KC-135 tanker during refueling over the Atlantic Ocean while returning from Reflex. The KC-135 also had no survivors.

1961 Flightline Torrejón Air Base, Madrid, Spain

Ann Margret at Torrejón AB, 1964 Stars and Stripes Newspaper

Torrejón AB Gate, 1953

The boom operators view from inside a KC-135 tanker as it refuels a B-47 over Spain

F-104 Starfighter Torrejón AB, 1961

F-104 Starfighter at Torrejón Air Base, April 1967

Open Day at Torrejón, 1963

Arrival of F-105B 57-5839 at Torrejón Air Base. Early 60's

Torrejón AB Main Exchange, 1972

NCO Club Torrejón AB, July 1972

View of Banco Hispano Americano late 1970

Air Force personnel standing in front of the Post Office building Torrejón Air Base, 1975

Torrejón Air Base Exchange Area – Circa, 1972

Torrejón Air Base Theater, 1984

BX Torrejón Air Base, 1984

BASE OPERATIONS Torrejón AB, 1973

Torrejón Air Base, 1973

F-14A Tomcat at Torrejón Air Base, June 1973

Control tower Torrejón AB, 1979

Main Gate, 1984

F-111 from RAF Lakenheath landing in Torrejón Air Base late 1980's

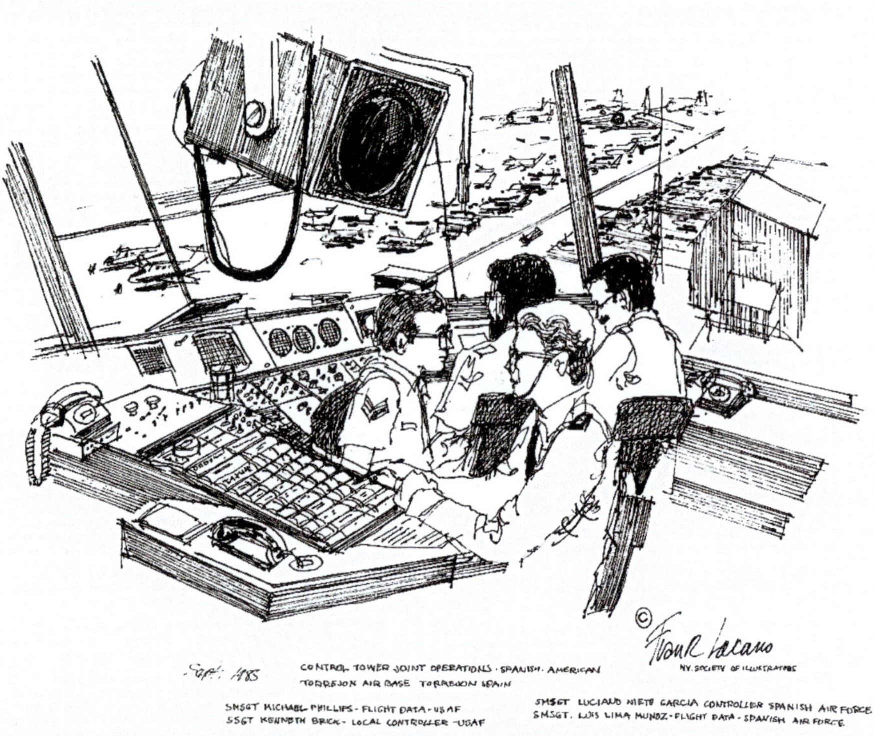

Torrejón AB Tower, September 1985

Torrejón Air Base Flight Line, 1986

Maj Gen Thomas Baker left and Maj Gen Winfield S Harpe the new 16th Air Force commander review the parade during the change of command ceremony at Torrejón Air Base, 1987

MATS (Military Air transport service) personnel in front of a Douglas C-124 Globemaster II at Torrejón Air Base. 1959

C-5 Galaxy Torrejon Flight Line, 1981

C-5 Galaxy ready for take off Torrejón Air Base, 1986

A view of a C-5 Galaxy from the wing of another one, 1988

C-5 Galaxy Torrejón AB Flight Line, 1988

C-141 in Torrejón AB, 1985

Torrejón Air Base C5 Galaxy mid 1980's

C-5 Galaxy approaching Torrejón Air Base, 1990

C-5 Galaxy just landed in Torrejón Air Base, 1991

C-5B Galaxy approching Torrejón AB, 1991

C-141 taking off from Torrejón Air Base, 1992

C-141 approaching Torrejón AB, 1990

C-141 arriving at Torrejón AB, 1990

C-141s at Torrejón AB, early 1980

Colonel Wade Paton and wife Ana Villarreal Garza Paton O'Club Torrejón

Manny Carazo with Stanley Jones, Thomas Hoffman, Michael Prado and some other friends ROAKS

Torrejón Air Base, 1991 (1)

Torrejón Air Base, 1991 (2)

Torrejón Air Base, 1991 (3)

Torrejón Air Base, 1991 (4)

Patches

PEACE THROUGH STRENGTH

BLUE KNIGHTS

RED FALCONS

418 BOMBARDMENT

PAX OPUS NOSTRUM

1000 HOURS
PHANTOM II

BEST IN USAFE
401ST TFW
SPAIN

CAELUM ARENA NOSTRA

KILLER BEES

612th TFS
613th TFS
614th TFS

FIGHTING 612TH

401ST AGS
KNIGHTS OF MAINTENANCE

401 CRS
MAINTENANCE MAGICIANS

401ST SUPPLY SQUADRON
HEART OF LOGISTICS

401st. CAMS

401ST EMS
DONE WITH PRIDE

401ST MMS
BEWARE OUR MIGHT

401ST TFW
F-16
TJ
TRANSFER TEAM

614TH TFS LUCKY DEVIL
QATAR
MAINTAINERS

614TH TFS LUCKY DEVILS
العراق
QATAR - ARABIAN GULF

626TH CAMS

600TH AIR BASE GROUP

AIR FORCE COMMUNICATIONS SERVICE

USAF HOSPITAL TORREJON

USAFE
FREEDOM'S
GUARDIAN

AFOSI DISTRICT 68
GUARDIANS OF THE MEDITERRANEAN

AFOSI DISTRICT 68
GUARDIANS OF THE MED

1000 FLIGHT HOURS
F-16 FIGHTING FALCON

F-16
Fighting
Falcon

Falconer

SAC
TORREJON
16

Printed by Amazon Italia Logistica S.r.l.
Torrazza Piemonte (TO), Italy

11827727R00165